LATE NIGHT SHOPPING

www.qheartland.com

Contents

TEMPLATES
- [ ] QS28 Log Cabin templates
      (Country Garden, **Prairie Flower**)
- [ ] QS32 Fan-tastic templates (Heirloom)
- [ ] SP1 Peaky & Spike & Friends templates
      (**Americana**, Storm at Sea, Perky Posies, Prairie Flower, From My Neck of the Woods)
- [ ] Pillow Template #412 65 97-01 or 15 square ruler
      (**Americana**)

NOTIONS
- [ ] QS56 Quick Grips
- [ ] Silk Pins
- [ ] STB Stiletto
- [ ] Small OLFA¤ Rotary Cutter
- [ ] 4 Gingher Pocket Scissor (Heirloom)
- [ ] Large and small mat boards
- [ ] Flannel Board
- [ ] 17 x 17 Q Snap Frame
- [ ] Fabric marking pencil
      (**Americana, Moon Over Montana,** Country Garden)
- [ ] .01 Permanent marking pen (Thread Painting)
- [ ] Water erasable marking pencil (Heirloom)
- [ ] Fade-Away Marking Pencil (Ribbon Embroidery)
- [ ] Free-Motion Guide Grip
- [ ] 1/4 wooden screw-type embroidery hoop
      (Thread Painting)
- [ ] Extension table for at surface
- [ ] Gimping Cord (Heirloom)
- [ ] Lace Shaping Board (Heirloom)
- [ ] Spray starch (Heirloom)
- [ ] Low-loft batting
- [ ] Trolley needle (Ribbon Embroidery)
- [ ] Snag-Nabbit tool (Ribbon Embroidery)
- [ ] Template plastic (**Moon Over Montana,** Country Garden)
- [ ] Applique Pressing Sheet (Country Garden)
- [ ] Light Box (Perky Posies)
- [ ] Fasturn (Prairie Flower)

NEEDLES
- [ ] Machine embroidery needle #75 (Thread Painting)
- [ ] 110 Universal needle (Heirloom)
- [ ] 2.0 / 70 twin needle (Heirloom)
- [ ] Size 80 (12) needle (Ribbon Embroidery)

THREADS
- [ ] 100% cotton thread
- [ ] 40 wt. embroidery thread (Thread Painting)
- [ ] Embroidery bobbin thread (Thread Painting)
- [ ] 60 or 80 wt. cotton thread (Heirloom)
- [ ] 40 wt. ecru Sulky¤ thread (Heirloom)
- [ ] 12 wt. Sulky¤ cotton thread
      (Heirloom, **Moon Over Montana,** Country Garden)
- [ ] YLI Wash-A-Way" thread (Heirloom)
- [ ] Sulky¤ Invisible thread (Ribbon Embroidery)
- [ ] Invisible mono lament thread (**Moon Over Montana**)

RULERS
- [ ] Omnigrid¤ Ruler 6 x 24
- [ ] Katie s Scallop Radial Rule (Heirloom, Country Garden)
- [ ] 15 square ruler or Pillow Template #412 65 97-01
      (**Americana**)

HUSQVARNA VIKING FEET
- [ ] Open-Toe Foot #412 27 70-45
      (**Americana**, Foundation Piecing, Heirloom, Storm at Sea
      Moon Over Montana, Country Garden, Perky Posies, **Prairie Flower**, From My Neck of the Woods)
- [ ] Open-Toe Stippling Foot #412 57 65-45
      (**Americana**, Thread Painting, Heirloom, **Moon Over Montana**, From My Neck of the Woods)
- [ ] Open-Toe Applique Presser Foot (Ribbon Embroidery)
- [ ] Dual Feed Foot
- [ ] Free-Motion Guide Foot #412 57 64-45 (Foundation Piecing)
- [ ] Gathering Foot #412 34 73-45 (Heirloom)
- [ ] Edge Stitching Foot #412 40 77-45 (Heirloom)
- [ ] Edge / Joining Foot #412 28 02-45 (Heirloom)
- [ ] 7 Groove Pin Tuck Foot #412 36 28-45 (Heirloom)
- [ ] Gimping Foot #411 85 09-45 (Heirloom)
- [ ] R Quilting Foot (Country Garden)

STENCILS
- [ ] ST-S Millenium Star quilt stencil (**Americana**)

MISCELLANEOUS
- [ ] Foundation by the yard (Foundation Piecing)
- [ ] 5/8 ecru French Insertion Lace (Heirloom)
- [ ] French Edging Lace with scalloped edge (Heirloom)
- [ ] Entredeux (Heirloom)
- [ ] 4 mm. and / or 7mm. silk ribbon (Ribbon Embroidery)

STABILIZERS
- [ ] Light-weight tear-away stabilizer (Thread Painting, Prairie Flower, From My Neck of the Woods)
- [ ] Tear Away Light Stabilizer by America Sews (Heirloom, **Moon Over Montana**, Country Garden, **Prairie Flower**, From My Neck of the Woods)
- [ ] Fuse N Tear Stabilizer by America Sews (Heirloom, From My Neck of the Woods)
- [ ] Ultra Solve or Romeo stabilizer (Heirloom)
- [ ] Sulky¤ Totally Stable Iron-on stabilizer (Ribbon Embroidery)
- [ ] Heat n Bond or Trans Web stabilizer
      (**Moon Over Montana**, Country Garden)

DISKS
- [ ] Husqvarna Viking Disks #24, #11, #17, #102, #48, Broderie Anglaise (Heirloom
- [ ] Husqvarna Palace Script Disk (Heirloom)

QUILTMAKING BASICS

HOW TO USE THIS BOOK
This book contains step-by-step instructions for each design.
A. Before starting, read through entire instructions so you get an idea of the complete process.
B. There are color photos to look at if picking fabric is difficult for you. Check yardage charts for each quilt before purchasing fabric. Make sure to prepare your fabric as suggested.
C. Templates are printed in actual size at the end of this book. Acrylic templates can be purchased at your local quilt shop or from "Quilting From The Heartland", P.O. Box 610, Starbuck, MN 56381 U.S.A. 1-800-637-2541 or 1-320-239-4044

PREPARATION OF ACRYLIC TEMPLATES

Templates come with protective paper on each side; simply peel off before using. They are pink in color (so you won't lose them in your fabric) as well as transparent which allows you to take advantage of certain fabric designs.

For best accuracy while cutting with the Rotary Cutter, apply Quick Grips to each corner of the template; if it's a larger template, put one in middle along edge. Quick Grips are small circles of felt with adhesive backing. They keep templates from sliding on your fabric while cutting. Please note! If you don't put the Quick Grips on the far corners, the fabric will move when you approach corner with cutter.

PREPARATION OF FABRIC
I prefer to use 100% cotton fabric because it is lightweight making it easy to quilt through three layers of the quilt sandwich. Cotton is easy to manipulate when matching points and flexible when working with curves. If you are going to use blends, choose all fabrics of the same blend.

Separate fabrics by color and wash in cool water with a mild soap that contains no bleaching additives. If fabric still bleeds after one washing, you may consider a second wash. Line or machine dry.

Caution! If you use a steam iron when you are piecing a quilt and you haven't pre-washed the fabric, your cut pieces will shrink unevenly, making working with them difficult.

PRESS AND STARCH
I have started to use spray starch on most fabrics that go into the quilt. Starch makes cutting and sewing much easier. It also acts as a stain guard, making it easier to remove pencil lines. A light mist is adequate for most quilting projects, but if pieces are small, spray both sides of fabric.

Starch will also prevent pieces from getting pulled into needle hole when sewing.

It is cheaper to mix your own starch with equal parts of Sta-Flo liquid starch and water. Put it in a mister and lightly mist fabric before pressing it.

GRAIN OF FABRIC
Lengthwise grain runs parallel to edge of fabric and crosswise grain runs from selvage to selvage. Both are considered to be on straight of grain. True bias is cut at a 45° angle and is stretchiest part of fabric. Avoid having bias edges of fabric on outside edge of quilt block. This will help keep quilt square; also, it will hang better if it is a wall quilt.

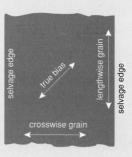

Occasionally I ignore this rule, especially if there is a design in the fabric that I want to capture. Because templates are transparent, you can place them in exact position before cutting. You can create some great designs, especially from border prints and stripes, but you can cut only one at a time. It will look as if a mouse has been into your fabric when you have finished cutting.

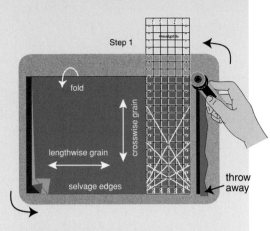

Step 1

fold

crosswise grain

lengthwise grain

selvage edges

throw away

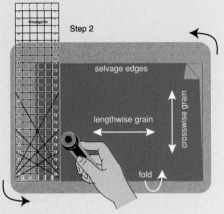

Step 2

selvage edges

lengthwise grain

crosswise grain

fold

VIKING OPEN-TOE 412-277045

100% COTTON

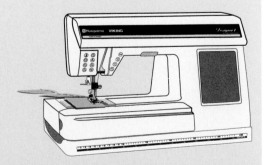

STRAIGHTENING FABRIC

Step 1. When same shapes are cut from more than one fabric used in the quilt, you can save time and accuracy by straightening more than one at the same time. Fold each fabric in half and place one on top of the other, lining up selvage edges. I like to work with folded fabric because layers seem to stabilize each other, especially if they are freshly ironed.

Place bottom edge of ruler on selvage edge. Start cutting about 1" from selvage edge going backwards off fabric. Starting in the same place, continue to cut away from yourself when trimming off uneven edges. Try not to disturb fabric after it is straightened. Bi-fold fabric on top of mat board before turning it.

CUTTING STRIPS WITH 6"X 24" RULER

Step 2. Move ruler to proper position to get width needed for strips. Cut required number of strips.

When you get more experienced with this method of straightening fabric and cutting strips, you can layer as many as six fabrics on top of each other.

If you are using a 6" x 12" Omnigrid® ruler, you will have to fold fabric in half matching selvage edges, and in half again. Note! Make sure your fabric is lying straight while cutting strips with the 6" x 12" ruler, so you don't end with zig zag strips.

After you have mastered cutting strips, it's easy to recut them into squares with a 6" x 12" ruler.

SETTING MACHINE FOR PIECING

I tell everyone that takes a class from me to make sure to sew all seams with a scant 1/4" seam allowance. This makes up for fabric used in seam line. Use scant 1/4" seam allowance for all quilt patterns that have 1/4" seam allowance included. I can't stress enough the importance of this rule.

On Designer I the scant 1/4" is found in Menu E-1. On Quilt Designer & Designer II it is #1 on E-1 stitch d-card.

THREAD AND FEET

I prefer to use an open-toe for piecing. On an open toe foot, the portion of foot directly in front of needle has been removed to give an unobstructed view of stitch.

Use 100% merc. cotton thread, size 50, to match 100% cotton fabric for care and strength. Cotton thread is strong, yet fine, for accurate piecing.

If you're using a Quilt Designer, Designer II or Designer I, don't forget to take advantage of the sensor foot pivot. Every time you stop, the needle goes down and the foot floats on any thickness. It is especially nice for chain sewing because you don't have to lift the presser foot each time you feed another set of pieces.

CHAIN SEWING

I chain sew pieces together whenever possible because it saves time and thread. At beginning and end of a seam, do not back stitch or cut thread. Feed next pair of pieces under presser foot as close as possible to first pair. Continue to feed pieces as close as possible. After all pieces have been sewn, remove chain and clip threads between pieces.

MACHINE QUILTING

Free motion quilting works best for continuous line designs, stippling, outlining flowers, and feathered designs.

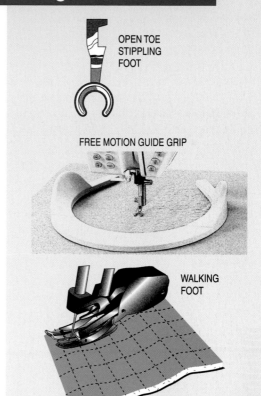

OPEN TOE STIPPLING FOOT

FREE MOTION GUIDE GRIP

Before attaching open toe stippling foot, take standard ankle and presser foot off the machine. Place open toe stippling foot on the presser bar. Screw in place with the accessory thumb screw. Lower the feed teeth and set presser foot pressure to the darning position. (For Designer I, Designer II, or Quilt Designer, select the V menu, touch free motion straight stitch V1). Place the Free Motion Guide Grip on quilt. Move it forward, backward and from side to side. Move quilt or fabric at a smooth pace for even stitches. Practice controlling speed of machine on fabric scraps before starting on a finished quilt top.

Because there is so much happening at one time, it's easy to get tense. Remember to breathe and relax when machine quilting. After all, this is fun!

Look where you're going, not at needle. If you sew too slowly, stitches will be long and if you sew too fast there will be too many stitches per inch. Practice improves your skills. Have fun with it. Just like hand quilting, every stitch won't be perfect.

WALKING FOOT

To sew straight lines, the walking foot works well. It can be used for cross hatching and stitching in the ditch. The machine will do the work and you will get perfect stitches.

DOES YOUR MACHINE EAT FABRIC?

Try one or more of these tips if you are having trouble with fabric getting pulled into feed dogs.

1. Switch to a single-hole needle plate.

2. Use an anchor cloth as a leader when starting to sew. Anchor cloth is a small square of fabric folded in half. Start sewing on anchor cloth and butt the next set of pieces up to it as you sew. Beginning stitches on patchwork will be more secure and won't pull apart as easily as first stitches sewn. Cut anchor cloth from beginning of your work and sew off onto it when ending. You won't have to hold threads when starting with this method. This will also save time and thread.

3. Spray starching fabric before cutting pieces stabilizes fabric and makes stitching easy.

SILK PINS

There is a big difference in pins. Some are as big as nails. I prefer glass head silk pins with a super fine .50mm steel shaft. They are fine and never leave holes. Silk pins slide easily into fabric because of the fine shank. Silk pins are best if it is necessary to sew over pins.

STILETTO

Use a stiletto instead of your pointer finger to guide fabric in front of needle when machine piecing. You won't worry about pieces scooting to one side at end of seam, when using a stiletto.

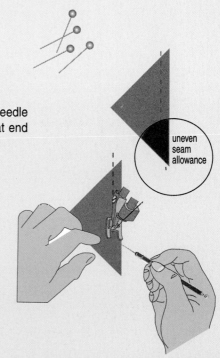

uneven seam allowance

PRESSING TECHNIQUE

There is a lot of debate about which way to iron seams when putting blocks together. There are advantages to both and I suggest you try both ways and decide for yourself which one you prefer. I don't necessarily use the fastest method, but I use the one that makes the block look best when finished. Sometimes both methods are used in the same quilt.

It is faster to iron seams to one side and seams are a little stronger, but you have more bulk in one place which makes it difficult to match some designs with triangles and hexagons. It takes more time to press seams open, but you will have a flatter quilt top making it easier to hand quilt. I will share with you which method I prefer for each quilt in this book.

No matter in which direction you iron seams, always take time to finger press seams first before ironing. It's much easier and you get better results when finger pressing on a hard surface. To finger press, use your pointer finger to scratch fabric in direction you want it to go as you move along seam allowance. Your finger will act as a mini iron and is often enough to do a good job. If your seam allowance does not lie flat, it's possible you didn't finger press it well. Finger pressing gives you added accuracy and speeds up ironing. It also eliminates pleats in seam wells.

After you have finger pressed seam, press it gently with a steam iron, always on wrong side. Sliding iron back and forth can cause bias edges to stretch, distorting block. Whichever method of pressing you use, be sure to press as you go. It is harder to match unpressed seams and crossing over them can cause seam wells at intersections.

If you press seams to one side, press seams towards darker fabric whenever possible to avoid shadows under light pieces.

Place a pressing mat near your sewing machine so you don't have to leave sewing area every time you want to press a seam. I don't use the large ironing board until blocks are being connected.

Much of the time I press pieces together before starting to sew. This creates a temporary bond of pieces making it easy to keep edges aligned as they are fed under the presser foot; then, finger pinning units together is enough.

PINNING OPTIONS

I'm sharing my favorite pinning techniques. Try both and use the one that works best for you. Accurate pinning is the key to getting seams perfectly matched. Seams are pressed open with both methods. Pressed-open seams take more time but the quilt will lie flat and hang straighter.

1. To make it easier to match seams pressed open, tip seam allowance in opposite directions.

2. Slide intersection seams together. Raised area of opposing seams helps to make a perfect match.

3. Without disturbing match, tip bottom seam allowance in same direction as top seam allowance and firmly hold in place. Secure match with pin on seam line through the **block**, not the seam allowance.

4. Pin is hidden when seam allowance is flipped open. Sew slowly when sewing over pin. Seam is stitched as an opened seam. The result is a flat block when pressed.

SECOND PINNING TECHNIQUE

5. Right sides together, put two rows together. Insert a pin 1/4" from edge through top and bottom. Leave this pin standing.

6. On both sides of standing pin, insert another pin through seam allowance to hold intersection in place. Remove standing pin before sewing.

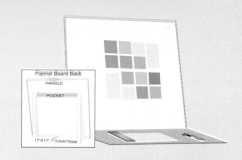

FLANNEL BOARD

Use a flannel board at cutting table when planning your next quilt. Mine has a pocket to insert a 17" x 17" Q-Snap frame to make it into an easel or a handle to hang on door or wall hook. It is easy to transport from cutting table to sewing machine or take to classes.

BORDERS

Every quilt needs one or more borders to announce its completion. Think of the border as a picture frame. If border fabric is plain, it becomes a showcase for quilting.

There can be one or more fabrics used in border which can be mitered or squared. I prefer the look of mitered corners unless there is a corner stone in the border. The corner stone can be a pieced block or a plain square.

When choosing the border, I lay strips of fabric along edge and use what feels right. Sometimes two borders look better than one. If you use two borders, they look best if they are of different widths. You might decide to introduce a large print in border that wasn't used in quilt.

When possible, pick quilting stencil before cutting borders so you know how wide to cut strips. It's easier to mark if you purchase matching border and corner sets. Make sure width of stencil fits within border. Last 1/4" of border around outside edge should not be counted because it will eventually be covered with binding.

BORDERS WITH MITERED CORNERS

Allow extra length for mitered corners. Measure distance from top to bottom on both sides of quilt. If your measurements are different, take average length. To find out how much extra is needed, fold cut strip on the diagonal. I cut strips 6 1/2" wide for most outside borders so I need an extra 13" (6 1/2" for each end). Next, subtract from top and bottom the 1/4" that is used in seam.

Match center of border strip to center of quilt edge. Hold in place with a pin. Insert another pin 1/4" from top and bottom end of quilt. Evenly insert more pins along edge. Sew this seam with quilt on top so intersections you want to sew over are visible. Stop sewing 1/4" from each corner on top and bottom of quilt. After all sides are attached, seams will touch in corners. Attach border on other side in same way. Repeat step to add top and bottom border.

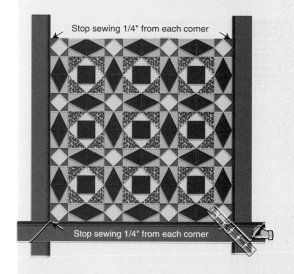

After all four sides have been attached, iron seam allowance towards border. Cross one border over the other making a perfect 90° corner. Make a chalk line on right side of both top and bottom at a 45° angle. Match these lines and pin to hold in place. Sew this seam starting at outside point and back stitch at inside corner. Corner should lie flat. Trim off excess fabric.

MARKING QUILTING DESIGN

Before making quilt sandwich, mark quilting designs on quilt top with a fabric marking pencil. Using pre-cut stencils is an easy, fast and economical way to transfer quilting designs. Plastic stencils have a series of slots, wide enough to allow points of pencils to mark through onto fabric. Bridges are left between slots to hold stencil together. You can join broken lines after stencil is removed to make a continuous quilting line or join them during quilting process.

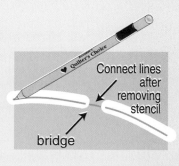

Consider open areas that need quilting. Quilting will show up more on a solid fabric than on a busy floral. If you use a fabric with very little print or even better, a solid, for back of quilt, it will be reversible. Choose stencil to complement quilt. Mark lightly through slots following lines until design is completed.

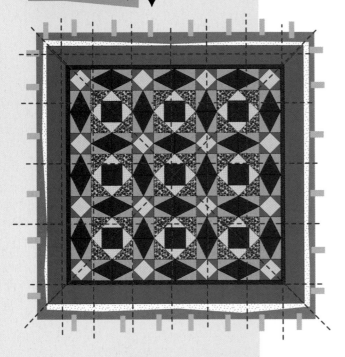

PREPARE QUILT BACK

If light fabrics were used in quilt top, don't use dark for quilt back because it will show through. Before making quilt sandwich (front, batting, and backing) you will need to make the quilt back. The back should be 2" - 3" larger (on all four sides) than pieced top. Measure finished quilt top and add 4" - 6" to length and width. If you are making a wall quilt less than 40" wide, you won't have to sew strips of fabric together for backing. Cut length needed. If quilt is wider than 40", you will have to sew strips together. Sew seams with a 5/8" seam allowance and trim to 1/4". Iron seam open.

Measure quilt top for which you are making the back and figure out best use of fabric. Length and width of quilt will determine whether you put seam lengthwise or crosswise. Center quilt over back and leave equal amounts of extra fabric on each side.

QUILT SANDWICH

After quilting design is marked on quilt top, make a quilt sandwich by placing back of quilt on bottom with wrong side facing up. The middle is batting and pieced quilt is on top, right side facing up. Work on a table top or a tile floor if available. Smooth out and secure bottom layer in place (wrong side facing up) with masking tape. Batting and pieced top is secured in place with pins.

I prefer low-loft batting for both hand and machine quilting. It's easier to get even stitches with light batting; also, finished quilts with this batting drape nicely over beds.

Baste quilt with a large needle diagonally, vertically and horizontally. You can also pin-baste with rust proof safety pins.

BASTING QUILT SANDWICH ON TABLE TOP

Fold top of quilt in half and mark center on all four edges. Do the same with batting and backing.

Mark center of table top in three places with a toothpick held in place by masking tape. Toothpicks make a bump that can be felt through quilt sandwich layers. If quilt is longer than length of table, put a tooth pick in center of table edge.

Fold back of quilt in half, wrong sides together. Match centers of back to toothpicks on table. Unfold back with wrong side up and secure ends with masking tape. If back is longer than table, secure it with clips.

Fold batting in half and match to center bumps. Let batting drape over table top.

Fold quilt top in half, right sides together and match fold to center bumps. Unfold quilt top over table top and smooth it out. Now you are ready to baste. Start in center and work your way out. If your quilt is larger than the table top, remove clamps after it is basted and readjust quilt sandwich on table top.

Turn excess backing along outside edge over batting and baste it in place with binding clips; you have a temporary binding. This prevents batting from getting snagged during quilting process.

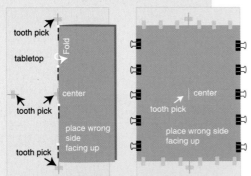

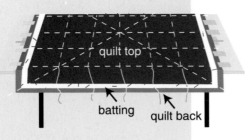

BINDING

To keep quilt and batting from shifting while you attach binding, machine sew with a walking foot or hand baste 1/8" from edge.

Cut enough 2" strips on the straight of grain or bias for binding.

Step 1. Cut off both ends of all 2" strips at a 45° angle. Now bulk of seam will be evenly distributed. Sew strips together and press seams open. At beginning, fold 1/4" back and press.

Step 2. Fold binding in half and press.

Step 3. Starting at end of binding with 1/4" folded back, place binding on right side of quilt. Make sure a seam does not fall on a corner; if it does, find a new place to start. Match edge of quilt to cut edge of binding. Start sewing 1" after 1/4" fold so end of binding can be slipped inside for a nice finish. Sew 1/4" from edge and stop sewing 1/4" from corner of quilt edge; back stitch. Cut thread.

Step 4. Turn your work and fold binding back. Binding edge and quilt edge should make a straight line when folded regardless of the angle of the quilt corner. This fold will start the miter on the corner.

Step 5. Place your finger on first fold and flip binding down to make the second fold even with binding; this will complete miter. Finger pin and start sewing from the outside edge to 1/4" of next corner. Repeat steps #3 - #5 until you are around entire quilt.

Step 6. Turn binding on the right side to back side of quilt to form miter.

Step 7. Fold other side over to complete mitered corner. Bulk in corners will automatically end opposite each other on top and bottom. Using a matching thread, hand sew with a blind stitch.

Hold binding in place with pins or binding clips as you stitch. If you use binding clips you won't have to worry about being poked with pins.

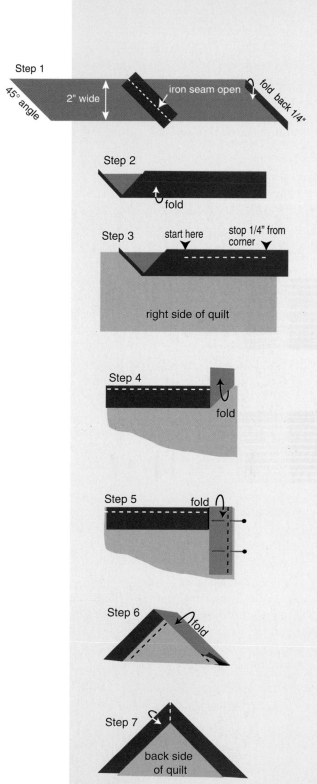

Step 1 45° angle 2" wide iron seam open fold back 1/4"

Step 2 fold

Step 3 start here stop 1/4" from corner right side of quilt

Step 4 fold

Step 5 fold

Step 6 fold

Step 7 back side of quilt

designed & pieced by Sharlene Jorgenson

machine quilted by Jean Johnson

Americana Yardage

finished size 49 1/2" x 49 1/2"

1 fat quarter for star centers

1/2 yd. binding

2/3 yd. border

1 1/2 yd. background fabric

3 yd. backing

five fat quarters of each color

I
INTERMEDIATE

SHOPPING LIST
SP1 Peaky and Spike templates
Fabric Grips
Small Rotary Cutter
Large and small Mat Board
Fabric marking pencil
6" x 24" Omnigrid® Ruler
Glass Head Silk Pins 0.05mm
Stiletto
Flannel Board
17" x 17" Q Snap Frame
15" sq. ruler or Pillow Template #412 65 97-01
Open Toe Foot #412 27 70-45
Open Toe Stippling Foot #412 57 65-45
ST-S Millennium Star quilt stencil

ABOUT AMERICANA

Step 1. A melting pot of patriotic red, gold and blue scraps creates a quilted tribute to all brave Americans. Movement was added by twisting and turning the stars.

It is easiest to pick background fabric on which the stars float before selecting fabrics for the stars. You can use fat quarters because the stars don't take very much fabric. I chose 5 red, 5 blue and 5 gold fat quarters with a variety of texture and background. The quilt looks scrappy because there isn't a definite arrangement. To keep the quilt from getting too confused and haphazard, I used the same gold around the square on point in the center of each block. On the blue blocks the star points are red and on the red blocks the star points are blue. I used both red and blue points on the gold blocks.

CUTTING INSTRUCTIONS

To straighten fabric see page 4.

Step 2. Templates A, D, G, H, and K from SP-1 Peaky & Spike & Friends are used to make the 12" finished blocks. Note! There are two tips when cutting for this quilt. It is very important all fabrics are right sides up. Place five fat quarters (fat quarters are18" x 22" pieces of fabric) on top of each other. It is also important to place template G and K exactly as shown in diagram so the angles of cut pieces match. Keep checking to see that nothing is turned around. This keeps all points on stars looking the same.

Line up edges on two sides of fat quarters. To get best use of your fabric follow the diagram. Note! There is only one H needed in center of each block so you will find just one in the second row. Even though my quilt doesn't have any gold points, the instructions tell you to cut them because they also look good on a blue or red background. Continue cutting from all color groups of fat quarters.

Step 1

12 1/2"

Step 2

TWIST AND TURN templates G and K, **DO NOT FLIP THEM**. They must be cut exactly as shown in diagram below.

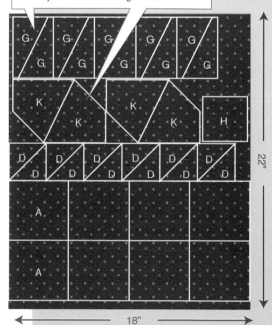

22"

18"

Step 3

Cut 36 gold D's

Step 3. I used the same gold to surround template H in all nine blocks. Make sure template D is placed on the strip as shown so bias is on longest edge. Cut 36 gold D's

SEWING INSTRUCTIONS

Step 4a. Right sides together, center bias edge of D on top of H. Ears should hang out evenly. Sew all seams with a scant 1/4" seam allowance (Menu E-1 quilt stitch on Husqvarna Viking Designer). Notice seam does not start in crevice. You should see a couple stitches on the triangle before hitting the square. I make the first stitches on an anchor cloth so beginning stitches on patchwork are as strong as center stitches sewn. Guide pieces in front of presser foot with stiletto to prevent pieces from scooting to one side at end of seam. Do not back stitch at beginning or end of seam.

Step 4 a.

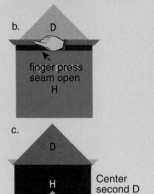

ANCHOR CLOTH

DO NOT BACK-STITCH

seam does not begin or end in crevice

b. Finger press seam open before pressing with an iron. It works much better to finger press on a hard surface before going to the ironing board. There is too much cushion on the ironing board and you risk the chance of getting pleats in the seam well.

c. Center second D on opposite edge of H. Sew seam.

d. Finger press seam open.

e. Attach D triangles to opposite edges of unit. The mouse ears will hang out evenly. This time, seam will begin and end in the crevice. Do not back stitch.

f. You will know it is right when the edges are straight and the points are 1/4" from the edge. Place template A (4 1/2" square) on top and trim off ears with rotary cutter. If you are a beginner and your seam allowance is too scant, extra fabric can be removed with second method. See diagram f.

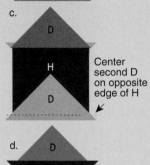

b. finger press seam open

c. Center second D on opposite edge of H

d. finger press seam open

because seam does not start in crevice there is a longer tail

e.

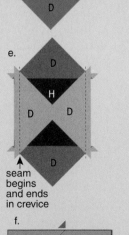

seam begins and ends in crevice

Make one of these units for the center of each nine-patch.

WEIRD ANGLES

Step 5. Diagram at right is the actual size of your unit. I wanted you to see clearly what happens at the end of each seam. Follow this guideline when pinning pieces K and G right sides together so you have something better than a happy accident. Seam begins and ends in crevice. Do not backstitch.

MATCH PIECES AS SHOWN

Step 5

G
WRONG SIDE

K
RIGHT SIDE

ACTUAL SIZE

SEAM STARTS IN CREVICE

f.

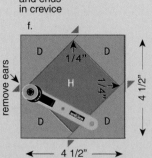

remove ears

1/4"

H

1/4"

4 1/2"

4 1/2"

Step 6. Finger press seam open.

Step 6

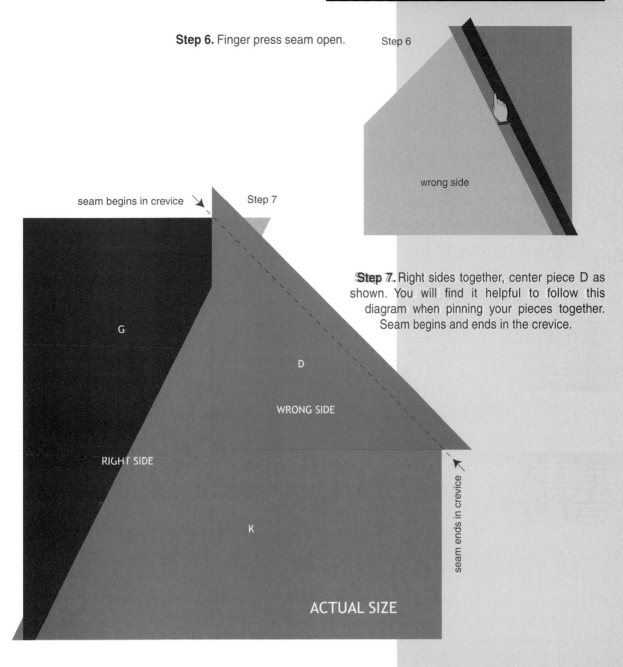

wrong side

seam begins in crevice

Step 7

G

D

WRONG SIDE

RIGHT SIDE

K

seam ends in crevice

ACTUAL SIZE

Step 7. Right sides together, center piece D as shown. You will find it helpful to follow this diagram when pinning your pieces together. Seam begins and ends in the crevice.

Step 8

Step 8a. Finger press seam open on wrong side.

b. Intersection should be 1/4" from edge. Place template A on top of unit and remove ears with rotary cutter. You should have a 4 1/2" square.

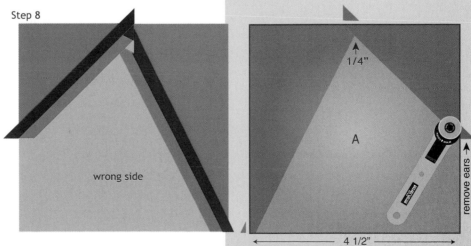

wrong side

1/4"

A

remove ears →

4 1/2"

Step 9

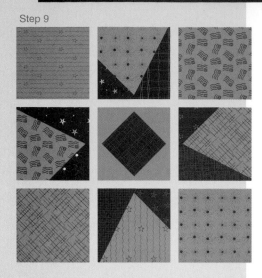

Step 9. Arrange 4 1/2" units on a flannel board as shown to make a nine-patch. I used both red and blue points in the stars with gold back ground.

Step 10. Connect units together into rows. Press seams open.

Step 10

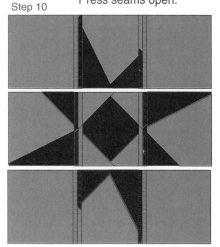

Step 11. See pinning techniques on page 6. Sew rows together. Press seams open.

Step 11

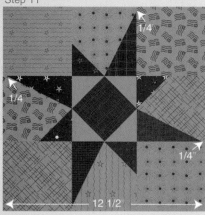

1/4"

1/4"

1/4"

12 1/2"

TWIST 'N TURN

I was introduced to Twist 'n Turn by Sharon Squier Craig and have used the technique often. If you don't want to twist 'n turn the blocks, set them into rows with sashing in between.

Step 12. Before starting to frame the blocks, arrange them to distribute the colors evenly. Five of my blocks twist to the left and four twist to the right. Next label them to twist right or left and separate them into piles.

Cut strips 2 1/2" wide from light background fabric to frame the blocks. Remove selvage edges from strips.

a. To twist to the left, place strip on upper right hand corner, right sides together. The corner of block should line up with end of strip. Begin sewing at corner and sew about half way down. Sew these seams with quilt block on top so intersections you want to sew over are visible. The first seam will always be a partial seam. Leave 2 1/2" or more extra length on strip. Finger press seam allowance open.

b. Add next strip to top and press seam open.

c. Add a strip on the left side and press seam open. Add the last strip to the bottom edge. Press seam open.

d. To complete the frame, finish first seam started in step a. Repeat this step to rest of blocks that twist to the left.

Step 12

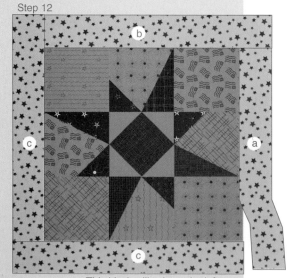

This block will twist to the left

ALTERNATE THE TWIST

Step 13a. To twist blocks to the right, place strip on bottom right corner. The bottom of the strip should line up with corner of block. Begin sewing at bottom right hand and stop sewing half way up. Leave 2 1/2" or more of extra strip length.

b. Add next strip to bottom and continue to work your way around the block. Press seams open as you go.

Step 13

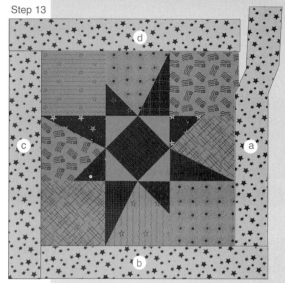

This block will twist to the right

Step 14. At this point you can set the blocks in straight rows or trim them so they twist and turn. I used the 14" line of the "Home Dec Pillow" template for marking the block to twist 'n turn. Line up the 14" corners of the pillow template with the seam lines best you can. Each corner should be equal. Follow the outside edge with a fabric marking pencil on all four corners. I suggest using the same pencil each time. If you don't have this template use a large square ruler.

Step 14

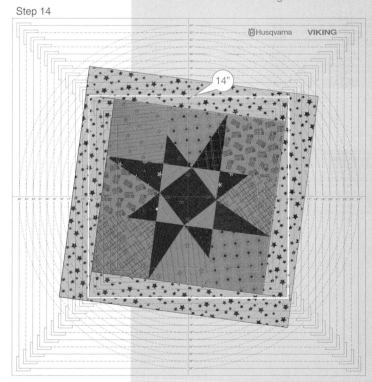

Step 15. Place ruler on line and cut the 14" square with a rotary cutter. This is a very forgiving method.

Step 15

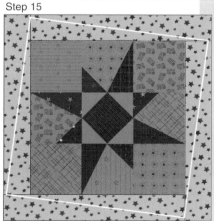

This block will twist to the left

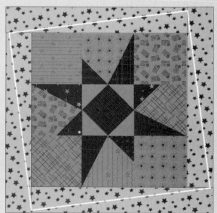

This block will twist to the right

Step 16. Connect blocks into rows. Press seams open.

Step 16

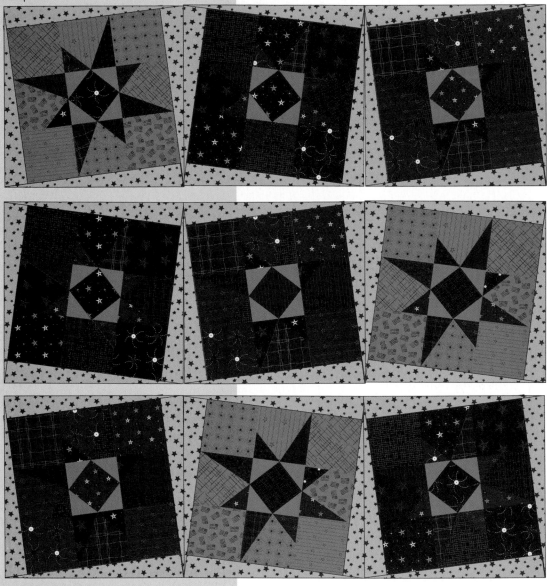

BORDERS

Step 17. Measure all four sides of the quilt. If measurements are different, take the average length. At this point my quilt measured 41" x 41". I cut four strips 4 1/2" wide x 41" long.

Attach borders to sides first. Press seams open. I decided to make four corner squares using the same block made in step 4. Attach a square on point unit to each end of two borders. Press seams open. Add top and bottom borders.

Step 17

Step 18

ST-S Millennium star stencil

Step 18. See pages 8 and 9 for finishing quilt.

The Millennium Star stencil was used in the border. We reduced the star pattern and used it on the light background between the blocks.

SULKY THREADS RAYON-40 WT.

1005-BLACK	1212-GREEN
1032-MEDIUM PURPLE	1226-BLUE
1127-CREAM	1296-PERIWINKLE
1039-RED	1517-DARK GREEN
1042-DARK BLUE	2104-VARIEGATED BLUE
1166-GRAY	2115-VARIEGATED GREEN
1183-ORANGE	2116-VARIEGATED TAUPE
1193-LIGHT PURPLE	2123-VARIEGATED RED
1195-DARK PURPLE	2134-VARIEGATED YELLOW

Humming A Spring Tune
designed & made by

Terry White

INTERMEDIATE

PRACTICE

Each item on the supply list is important and can make a difference in your free motion embroidery experience.

Put fabric and stabilizer in hoop, taut. Fabric is put in hoop opposite way from hand embroidery-with fabric against the sewing machine.

Lower feed dogs. Put your hoop under the needle and draw bottom thread up through fabric. Holding both threads, take a few stitches in one place.

TUG TOP THREAD TO POP BOBBIN THREAD THROUGH QUILT LAYERS

Cut loose threads. Start sewing at a slow speed and move the hoop around in circles. You will feel tension between the fabric and needle. If you move the hoop too fast, you may break a needle. If you move it too slow your stitches may be too small. Now increase the speed of your machine and begin to move the hoop at a steady, even pace. You will begin to feel that you are getting a rhythm to your movements. This may seem like handwriting lessons you took when you were little. Make some sweeping movements back and forth. If your machine doesn't like back and forth, try side to side.

Once you have achieved smooth curved lines, and you feel the control, practice outlining and filling in a simple drawing. Practice various stitches in the diagrams on page 20. Practice writing your name in cursive.

Free-motion quilting is basically the same as free-motion embroidery. You want to use a quilting needle. Cotton fabrics and batting are best-you will avoid skipped stitches. You can use rayon embroidery thread or metallics in the needle and regular dressmaking threads in the bobbin. Practice making long open stippling stitches on a sample.

SUPPLIES FOR FREE-MOTION EMBROIDERY
- 100% medium weight, even weave cotton fabric
- Light-weight tear-away stabilizer
- 1/4" wooden screw-type embroidery hoop
- Open toe stippling foot
- Machine embroidery needle #75
- 40 wt. embroidery thread
- Embroidery bobbin thread
- Extension table or cabinet for flat surface
- .01 Permanent marking pen

Tips for full control of where your needle goes when doing free motion embroidery:
- Lower feed dogs
- Use a straight stitch
- Set sewing machine to darning setting. If you have a Husqvarna Viking Designer I, Designer II, or Quilt Designer, select V menu; then touch special stitches V1.
- Use Open-Toe Stippling Foot so you can see where you're stitching.
- Put fabric and stabilizer in hoop, taut. Fabric is put in hoop opposite way from hand embroidery-with fabric against surface of the sewing machine.

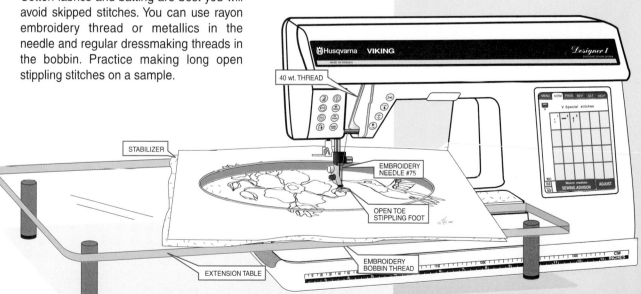

STABILIZER

40 wt. THREAD

Husqvarna VIKING
MADE IN SWEDEN

Designer I
EXCLUSIVE SENSOR SYSTEM

EMBROIDERY NEEDLE #75

OPEN TOE STIPPLING FOOT

EXTENSION TABLE

EMBROIDERY BOBBIN THREAD

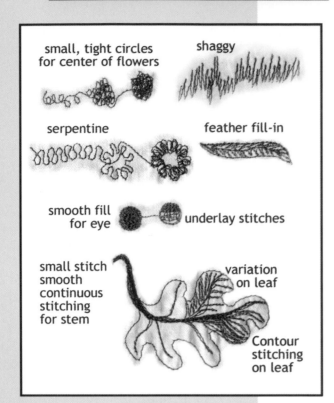

small, tight circles for center of flowers

shaggy

serpentine

feather fill-in

smooth fill for eye

underlay stitches

small stitch smooth continuous stitching for stem

variation on leaf

Contour stitching on leaf

MAKING TEXTURES WITH STITCHES

Different textures can be achieved with a straight stitch on your machine in free-motion embroidery. Once you have established control of your stitching, you can draw, fill in various textures and threads, and blend colors.

Practice making each of the stitches shown in the diagram to the left to give you confidence before making flowers and birds. Notice how Terry made underlay stitches on the eye before filling it in to get a smooth flat surface.

ABOUT HUMMING A SPRING TUNE

Terry combined my favorite bird and hobby into this wall quilt. She first made sketches of each part and then combined them on a light box. She uses her sketches for reference when free-motion painting. She also suggests looking at color photos to get more details.

PREPARATION OF QUILT BLOCK

Cut all blue strips 1 1/2" wide. Refer to diagram for length of each blue strip. Cut rest of pieces for block the sizes shown in the diagram. Sew all pieces together with a scant 1/4" seam allowance. Press seams open.

With a water erasable fabric pencil trace design onto each block. Use a light box for tracing the design. Three blocks are for thread painting and green blocks are for machine quilting. Use green thread a shade darker than the fabric so the quilting shows.

31 1/2" x 31 1/2"

Humming A Spring Tune
YARDAGE

- 1/2 YARD (BLOCKS & BINDING)
- FAT QUARTER
- FAT QUARTER
- FAT QUARTER
- 1/3 YARD
- 1/2 YARD

1 YARD BACKING

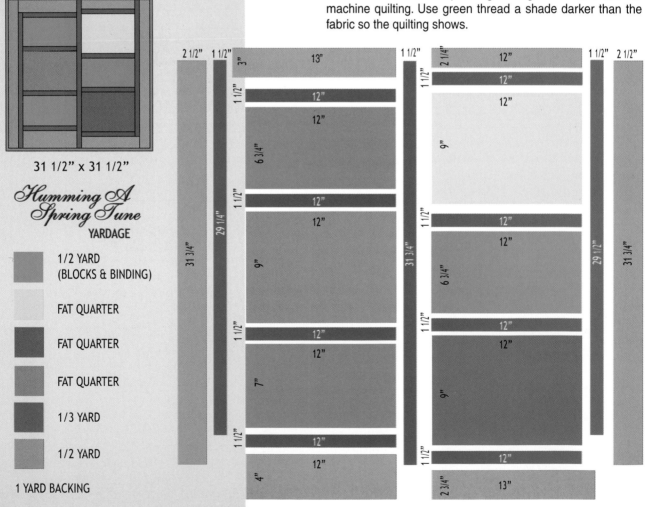

FLOWER COLORS
PURPLE FLOWER
1195-DARK PURPLE (outline petals and buds)
1296-PERIWINKLE (outer edge of petals)
2115-VARIEGATED GREEN (fill in leaves)
1517-DARK GREEN (outline leaves and stems)
1032-MEDIUM PURPLE (fill in petals and buds)
1193-LIGHT PURPLE (highlight petals)
2123-VARIEGATED RED (circle around center)
2134-VARIEGATED YELLOW (center)

RED FLOWER
1039-RED (outline flower and buds)
2123-VARIEGATED RED (petals fill in and leaves fill in)
1183-ORANGE (circle around center)
2134-VARIEGATED YELLOW (center)
1517-DARK GREEN (outline leaves)
2115-VARIEGATED GREEN (fill in leaves and stems)

BLUE FLOWER
1226-BLUE (outline of petals and buds)
1042-DARK BLUE (fill in of petals and buds)
2104-VARIEGATED BLUE (fill in petals)
2123-VARIEGATED RED (circle around center)
2134-VARIEGATED YELLOW (center)

MAKING FLOWERS, LEAVES AND STEMS

1. Trace pattern found on page 23 onto your fabric with a fabric marking pencil. Outline petals with a smooth line, then partially fill in petals by drawing lines with thread to describe the shape and veins in the petals. The second color of purple fills in the petal between first lines of stitching and blends colors.

2. Next, use variegated red thread, drawing in a serpentine fashion around the center of flower. Go over this area 3 times with the same serpentine stitch.

3. Using variegated yellow thread inscribe tiny circles around entire center, overlapping to achieve a French Knot look.

4. Next, flower is outlined with a dark thread, veins are drawn, and red part of flower is outlined.

5. Draw outline and veins of buds. Use either smooth stitching or a longer stitch for a more natural look. Fill in with second color between first lines of stitching with a smooth, shorter stitch.

6. Outline leaves with dark green using a smooth short stitch. Use variegated green to fill in with contour stitching. Notice, you will get a striped effect if you fill in back and forth. If you watch for the color changes, you can manipulate the color you want in each section. You can mix darks and lights for a more mottled look, or you can do the stitching in side by side lines to get a more striped effect. You can also stitch little areas of one color, then move onto another section and fill in with the next color.

7. Straight stitch stems in green with a smooth small stitch, stitching lines side by side to fill in.

BIRD THREAD COLORS
2115-VARIEGATED GREEN
1127-CREAM (belly and outline of eye)
2116-VARIEGATED TAUPE (feathers and lower body)
1166-GRAY (beak)
1005-BLACK (eyes and feet)
1212-GREEN (outline)

MAKING HUMMINGBIRDS
Start with variegated green to fill in the top of the head and top of wings. Use long, shaggy stitches to fill in these areas. Go back and forth so variegated threads mix and a natural coloration is achieved.

Next use cream colored thread to outline the eye. Just stitch around the eye several times to fill in, then fill in the center of the body with long shaggy stitches.

Use variegated taupe for feathers and bottom section of body. Draw feathers with alternating diagonal lines, giving the impression of feathers. Fill in tail feathers in same manner. Bottom section of body is done in long, shaggy stitches, stitching into cream color area with long and short stitches for a natural blending.

Use variegated red to fill in throat with shaggy stitches.

Use black to fill in eye by sewing straight horizontal lines. Draw the feet with black.

Outline the whole bird with grey-green thread and a smooth line of stitching.

APPLIQUE LEAVES
Trace leaf and bud patterns below onto smooth side of Trans-web™. Iron Trans-web™ to wrong side of fabric. Cut out green leaves and orange flower bud on the pencil line. Iron leaves and flower onto corners of quilt block as shown in picture on page 18.

Applique with a satin stitch using matching threads. If you have a Quilt Designer, Designer II, or Designer I, use the needle stop down so the foot pops up making it easy for you to pivot.

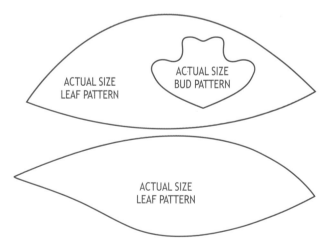

ACTUAL SIZE LEAF PATTERN

ACTUAL SIZE BUD PATTERN

ACTUAL SIZE LEAF PATTERN

See pages 8 and 9 for instructions on finishing your quilt.

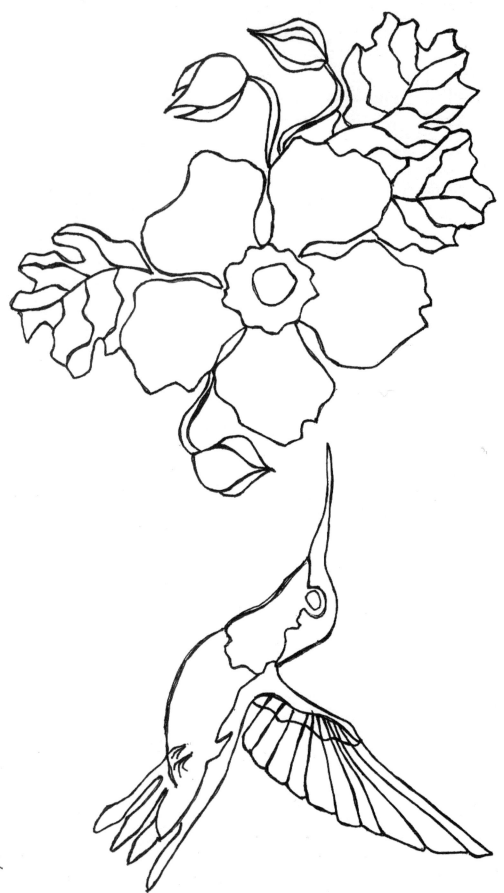

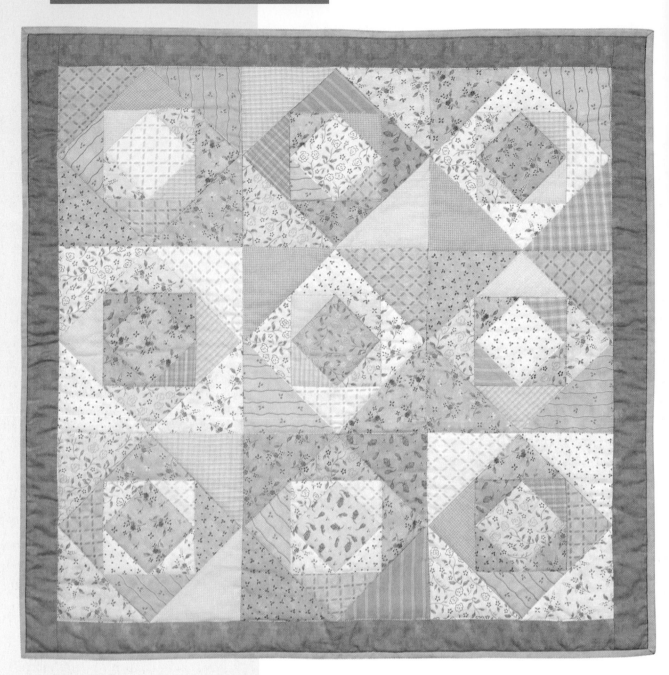

SQUARE-IN-A-SQUARE
Queen size
132 Foundation by the Yard blocks
1 yd. of 16 prints
3 yds. border
9 yds. backing

SQUARE-IN-A-SQUARE
Wall Quilt *(finished size 40" x 40")*
9 Foundation by the Yard blocks
16 fat quarters
1/2 yd. border
1 1/3 yd. backing

**designed & pieced by
Brittany Tostenson**

**machine quilted by
Jean Johnson**

FOUNDATION PIECING

SHOPPING LIST
Foundation by the yard
Small Rotary Cutter
Large and small mat board
Glass head silk pins 0.05mm
6" x 24" Omnigrid® ruler
Open toe foot 412 27 70-45
Free motion guide foot 412 57 64-45
Flannel board
17" x 17" Q Snap frame

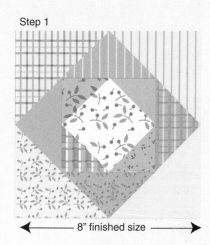

Step 1

← 8" finished size →

ABOUT SQUARE IN A SQUARE
Step 1. Brittany chose pastels to match her bedroom for this quilt. She chose to make it look scrappy so she started in the center each time with a different fabric. She also alternated colors in each block. In this block the first round is green, second round is pink, and the last round is yellow. Make all blocks and arrange them to distribute the colors evenly. Each block is an 8" finished square.

CUTTING INSTRUCTIONS FOR EACH BLOCK
Step 2. Cut one 5" square for each center.

Cut four 2 1/2" x 4 1/2" rectangles from different prints for first trip around center square.

Cut four 3" x 6" rectangles from different prints for second trip around the center square on point.

Cut four 6" squares for last trip around the center. To save fabric, Brittany cut them in half diagonally. Because you cut the squares in half there is enough for two blocks.

To save time, place four strips on top of each other when cutting squares and rectangles.

Brittany cut all of these pieces from each color and made piles at the sewing machine so it was easy to make each block different.

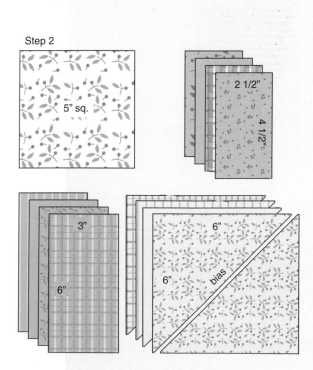

Step 2

5" sq.

2 1/2"

4 1/2"

3"

6"

6"

6"

bias

Step 3

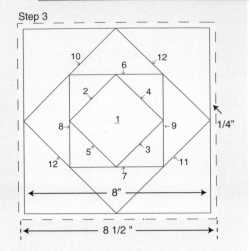

Step 3. Cut the 'Foundation By The Yard' apart into 8 1/2" squares following the long dashed lines.

Step 4

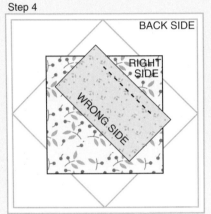

Step 4. Turn the square over to the "wrong" side. This is the side on which the colored quilt fabric will be placed. When the block is finished, this will be the "right" side.

Place a 5" square over the #1 area. It should extend over the lines by at least 1/4". Place the quilt fabric with the wrong side against the wrong side of the printed foundation square. Pin the square in place. If you are unsure of the placement, hold it up against a light.

Find where piece #2 goes. Right sides together, place a 2 1/2" x 4 1/2" rectangle to cover the area. Place the piece over piece #1 right sides together so it extends over the stitching line with the #2 arrow. Pin in place out of the way of sewing line.

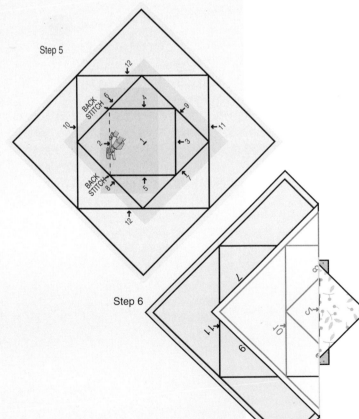

Step 5. Turn the square over, and stitch on the #2 line. Set the machine for center needle position and use an open toe foot so you can see exactly where you are going.

Backstitch at beginning and end of seam line or use the fix at beginning and end of seam if you have that option. Do not sew past the end of line. Turn square back to wrong side. Be sure the #2 fabric covered the #2 area with at least 1/4" extending over the line.

Step 6. Fold the foundation piece over to the left, along the stitching line.

Step 7. Brittany likes to use the Add-A-Quarter™ ruler which is designed for foundation piecing. It has a 1/4" lip which makes it easier for cutting away excess fabric. Position the Add-A-Quarter™ (lip side down) snugly against the fold. Cut away excess fabric. Do not cut into the foundation piece. If you don't have a ruler with a lip, place any ruler on top with 1/4" extended over the seam.

Step 7

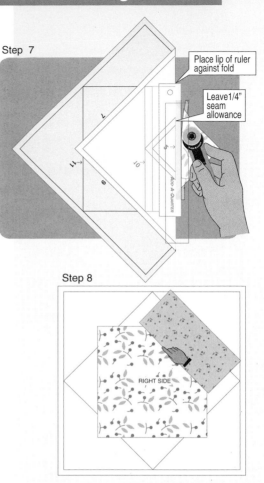

Place lip of ruler against fold

Leave 1/4" seam allowance

Step 8. Finger press the rectangle away from center square before pressing with an iron.

Step 8

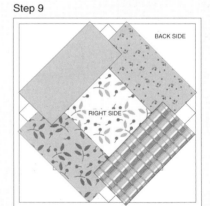

RIGHT SIDE

Step 9. Finger pin second rectangle in place (opposite the first rectangle). The seams are numbered. Continue until you have four 2 1/2" x 4 1/2" rectangles attached. Finger press seam allowance away from center and trim off excess fabric each time a new rectangle has been added.

Step 9

BACK SIDE

RIGHT SIDE

Step 10. Next add four 3" x 6" rectangles repeating the same process.

Step 10

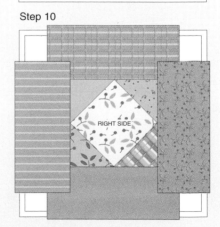

RIGHT SIDE

Step 11

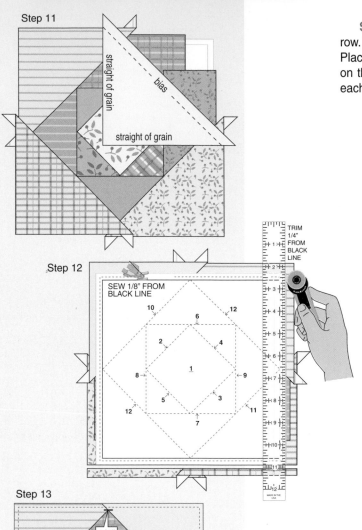

Step 11. Triangles are added to make the last row. The process is the same using a different shape. Place the bias edge of triangle as shown. Sew seam on the back side of block on the line. Press and trim each time a new triangle has been added.

Step 12

Step 12. Turn the block to the wrong side and sew 1/8" outside black line to keep pieces from shifting when connecting blocks.

Place ruler on top of block and match 1/4" line on ruler with black line on block. Trim off excess fabric with rotary cutter.

Step 13

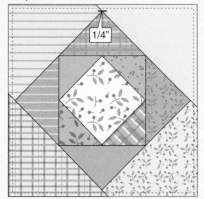

Step 13. Note! The intersections are 1/4" from the edge after edges have been trimmed.

Step 14

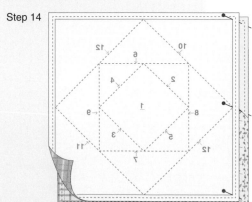

CONNECTING BLOCKS INTO ROWS

Step 14. After all blocks have been made, arrange them to distribute the colors evenly. Right sides together, insert a pin at 1/4" intersection through the top and bottom. Put another pin at beginning and end of seam. Sew on black line. Press seams open.

Step 15

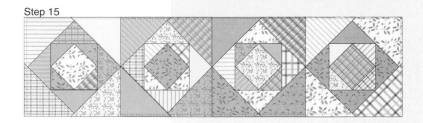

Step 15. The size of a quilt is determined by number of blocks in a row and number of rows you connect; With each added block quilt grows 8". Press all seams open.

Step 16. Add a 3" border to the wall quilt (6" border to queen size).
Page 7 has more border options.
Page 8 Quilt sandwich.
Page 5 setting machine for quilting. Quilt 1/4" from edge of each piece.
Page 9 binding.

Step 16

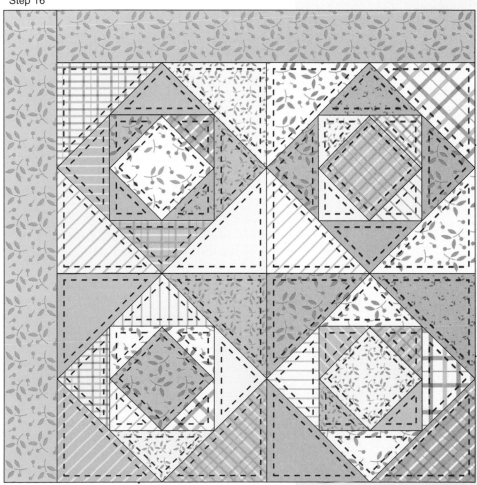

HL
designed
and
made by
Connie
Palmer

machine
quilted by
Linda
Tailor

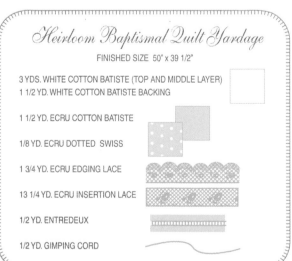

Heirloom Baptismal Quilt Yardage

FINISHED SIZE 50" x 39 1/2"

3 YDS. WHITE COTTON BATISTE (TOP AND MIDDLE LAYER)

1 1/2 YD. WHITE COTTON BATISTE BACKING

1 1/2 YD. ECRU COTTON BATISTE

1/8 YD. ECRU DOTTED SWISS

1 3/4 YD. ECRU EDGING LACE

13 1/4 YD. ECRU INSERTION LACE

1/2 YD. ENTREDEUX

1/2 YD. GIMPING CORD

ABOUT THE BAPTISMAL QUILT

Connie used ecru and white Swiss cotton batiste, French lace combined with heirloom techniques to create this beautiful baptismal quilt. Connie made the quilt to resemble a cathedral window. Each section of window shows off different heirloom techniques. Covered in this quilt are: no pin lace shaping, free form lace shaping, madeira applique, entredeux, puffing, folded tucks, pintucks, and machine embroidery. In center window pane her grandchild's name is embroidered with an ecru rayon thread. The baptismal date is embroidered in the center of the heart.

Linda Tailor machine quilted the majority of open areas with feathers and filled the outside border with tear drops surrounded by echo quilting.

SHOPPING LIST

Water erasable marking pen	Stiletto
Gathering foot Husqvarna Viking 412-34-73-45	4" Gingher pocket scissor
Edge Stitching Foot Husqvarna Viking 412-40-77-45	8" x 12" mat board cutting board
Edge Joining Foot Husqvarna Viking 412-28-02-45	Small rotary cutter
7 Groove Pin Tuck Foot Husqvarna Viking 412-36-28-45	5/8" ecru French insertion lace (with header thread)
Open toe stippling foot Husqvarna Viking 412-57-65-45	French edging lace with scalloped edge
Open toe foot Husqvarna Viking 412-27-70-45	Entredeux
Gimping Foot Husqvarna Viking 411-85-09-45	Spray starch
60 or 80 wt. cotton thread	Tear Away Light Stabilizer by America Sews
40 wt. ecru Sulky® thread	Fuse 'N Tear Stabilizer by America Sews 141 000822
12 wt. ecru Sulky® cotton thread	Ultra Solve or Romeo stabilizer
YLI Wash-A-Way™ thread	Katie's Scallop Radial Rule™ Mini size
Gimping cord	Low-loft batting
110 Universal needle	QS 32 Fan-tastic Fan templates
2.0 / 70 twin needle	Husqvarna Viking embroidery Disks 24,11,17, 102
Lace shaping board	and
Glass head silk pins	48 Broderie Anglaise
	Husqvarna Viking Palace Script Disk

PIN TUCKS

Cut an 18" x 10" rectangle of white cotton batiste for the heart block if you want background to be filled with pin tucks. Do not spray starch the fabric, just press it.

Step 1. Put 2.0 twin needle on machine and thread with two spools of 60 wt. thread. Follow your machine guide book to thread the twin needle.

Step 2. Make a straight line with water erasable fabric marking pen because the first tuck must be straight.

Step 3. Use 7 groove pin tuck foot. Put needle in center needle position. Set stitch length at 1.5. Stitch first pin tuck. Tucks are formed by twin needle sewing as fabric tunnels into groove on underside of foot.

Step 4. To make pin tucks a little farther apart, Connie used the edge of her presser foot as a guide to sew second pin tuck. See diagram. Sew 45 tucks. If you want pin tucks closer together, place first pin tuck into one of the grooves of the pin tuck foot.

FOLDED TUCKS

Step 1. Cut two pieces of white cotton batiste 9" x 16". Use a water erasable marking pen to draw parallel lines 2" apart. These lines mark fold lines.

Step 2. Fold fabric on line. If you can adjust needle position, move it all the way to the left. Place flange of edge stitching foot on edge of fold and stitch or sew approximately 3/8" from edge. These tucks were all pressed to go same direction. Repeat to make second block. Trim both blocks to 8" x 9".

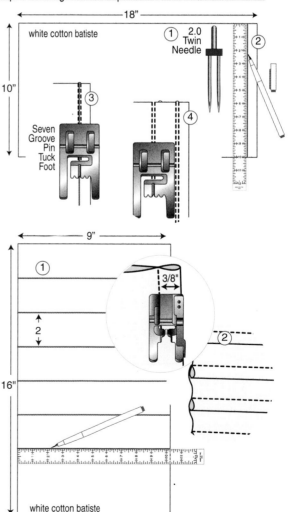

NO PIN LACE SHAPING BLOCK

1 yd. insertion lace

Step 1. See how to make pin tucks on page 31. With a water erasable fabric marking pen, trace heart onto a rectangle of pin-tucked fabric. Find pattern on page 43. Draw a bisecting line through center of heart.

Step 2. Cut piece of French insertion lace 4" longer than length needed to go around heart. Using an A foot, baste heart in place with zig zag stitch (1.5 width and 1.5 length) along outside edge of heart with a 60 or 80 weight cotton thread. You can use the no pin lace shaping technique to make any shape.

Start sewing along outside edge at center top of heart template 2" from end of lace. Inside edge of lace will be wavy. Continue sewing to bottom point. Leave needle in down position to hold lace while pivoting.

If you have a Husqvarna Viking Quilt Designer, Designer II or Designer 1, use needle stop down so the foot pops up making it easy for you to pivot. If you don't have that feature, stop with needle down at bottom point and pivot.

When sewing opposite side, a miter will appear at bottom center point. Continue sewing along curve and stop at top center.

Step 3. Fold in miter at bottom of heart. Next, pull header threads on inside of heart to make lace lie flat.

Step 4. Make a miter at center top by folding lace. Pin to hold. Lightly mist with starch and press to hold curves. When pressing, don't slide the iron back and forth. Instead pat (up and down) lace heart with an iron so lace will lie flatter.

Step 5. With a Gingher pocket scissor or another scissor with blunt ends, trim fabric from behind the heart half the width of the lace.

Step 6. To fill the heart, Connie suggested an embroidered bow (design 12 from Husqvarna Viking Disk 48, Broderie Anglaise, designed by Kathy Harrison), pin tucks, or the child's baptismal date (Palace script disk 12 mm). Embroidery was done with 40 wt. ecru rayon thread on ecru dotted swiss.

Center heart over embroidered bow or embroidered date and pin to hold in place. Zig zag along inside edge of lace. Cut away excess fabric from behind the heart half width of lace.

Step 7. With an open toe foot and a 110 universal needle, sew the pin stitch along both edges of insertion lace with a 80 wt. cotton thread. Use pin stitch L-2.5 W-2.0 (menu D stitch 46 on Husqvarna Viking designers).

Trim rest of fabric from behind insertion next to pin stitch with a pocket scissor. After you have removed fabric from behind lace, zig zag on miter, then trim lace tab away from miter.

Step 8. Embroider design 8 from disk 24 on each side of heart. Use a Tear Away Light Stabilizer behind embroidery. Trim block to 15" x 8 1/4".

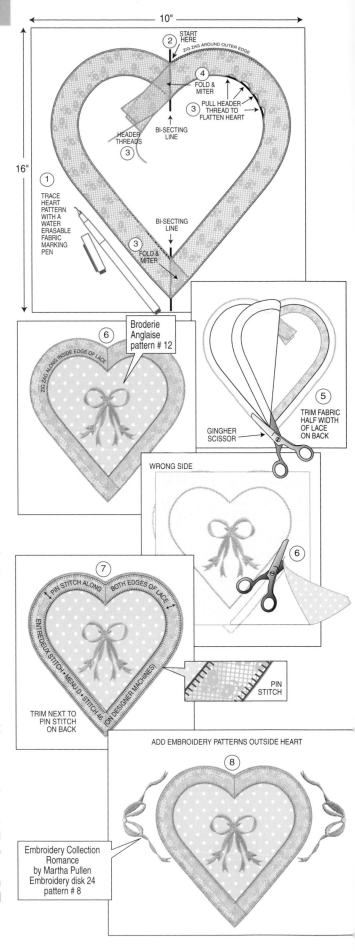

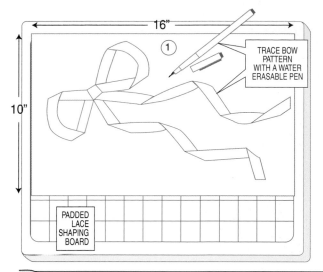

16"

10"

1

TRACE BOW
PATTERN
WITH A WATER
ERASABLE PEN

PADDED
LACE
SHAPING
BOARD

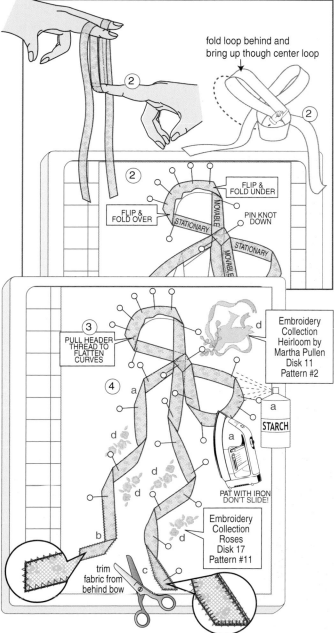

2

fold loop behind and
bring up though center loop

2

2

FLIP &
FOLD UNDER

FLIP &
FOLD OVER

PIN KNOT
DOWN

MOVABLE

STATIONARY

STATIONARY

MOVABLE

3

PULL HEADER
THREAD TO
FLATTEN
CURVES

4

a

d

Embroidery
Collection
Heirloom by
Martha Pullen
Disk 11
Pattern #2

a

STARCH

a

PAT WITH IRON
DON'T SLIDE!

d

d

d

d

d

Embroidery
Collection
Roses
Disk 17
Pattern #11

b

trim
fabric from
behind bow

c

FREE FORM LACE SHAPING BLOCK

1 1/4 yd. insertion lace

Step 1. Making a bow with free form lace shaping can be done with or without a pattern. You need to work on a padded lace shaping board. With a water erasable fabric marking pen, trace bow onto a 16" x 10" piece of fabric or pin fabric over a paper template. Find bow pattern on page 40.

Step 2. Cut 1 1/4 yd. of French insertion lace with a header on both edges. Find center of lace and make two loops. Tie a bow like you would tie a shoe lace.

Pin knot down catching just edge of knot so ends can still be moved while shaping bow. Find stationary and movable parts of loop on each side of knot. Starting with stationary loop, pin bow in place with glass head pins following traced bow. Place outer edge of lace along outer template line. Insert pins along outside edge of header at an angle to hold lace in place. Put a pin every 1/2" to 3/4" apart. Flip lace to form the miter on inside curve of bow. Inside edge of lace on curve will be wavy. On second corner, fold lace under to make a miter. Pull on movable end to get rid of extra lace. Continue shaping lace on both sides of bow template. Let loose ends extend below bow.

Step 3. Next pull header threads to make inside curves lie flat.

Step 4a. Flip flop tails of lace back and forth to create miters. Pin to hold. Lightly mist with starch and press to hold curves and miters. When pressing, don't slide the iron back and forth. Instead, pat (up and down) the bow with an iron.

b. If you have a Quilt Designer, Designer II or Designer 1, use the needle stop down so the foot pops up making it easy for you to pivot. If you don't have that feature, stop with needle down on curves and points before you pivot. Using an A foot baste bow in place with zig zag, stitch (1.5 width and 1.5 length) along outside edge with a 60 or 80 weight cotton thread.

Use 110 universal needle and open toe foot to sew pin stitch, L-2.5 W-2.0 (menu D stitch 46 on Designers) along both edges of lace.

c. With a Gingher pocket scissor (has blunt ends) trim fabric from behind the bow. Leave folded-over edges of lace for strength.

d. Connie added embroidery for more embellishment on bow block. Position lace bow over embroidery template that matches the design you have chosen and draw registration marks with water erasable pen. Put a tearaway light stabilizer behind bow and embroider with a contrasting ecru 40 wt. rayon thread.

Trim bow block to 15" x 8 1/4".

FAN BLOCK

**1/2 yd. Entredeux
1 1/2 yd. insertion lace
1 yd. edging lace**

Step 1. Cut one strip of white Swiss cotton batiste 6" x 18" long and one strip of ecru dotted Swiss 6" x 18" long. Cut each strip in half diagonally. Take half of each strip and sew the halves together diagonally. Press seam allowance to one side. You will have one extra set of diagonal strips to make a matching fan pillow.

Step 2. Trim seam allowance to 1/8". Using an A foot, baste lace insertion over seam allowance with a zig zag stitch (1.5 length and 1.5 width).

Step 3. Attach Open Toe foot. (Open Toe foot has a tunnel on bottom side which makes it easier to feed fabric when there is a thread buildup.) Use a 110 Universal needle and 60 or 80 weight cotton thread to do pin stitch, L-2.5 W-2.0 (menu D, stitch 46 on Husqvarna Viking Designers) along both edges of lace. The 110 needle is kinder to lace than wing needle.

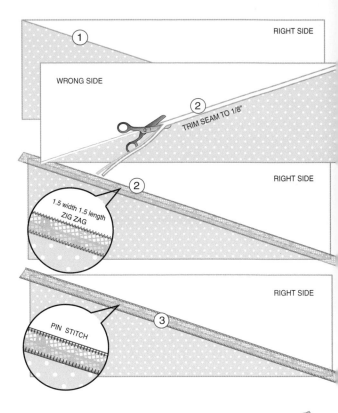

Step 4. With Gingher pocket scissor (a scissor with blunt ends) trim fabric from behind lace right next to pin stitching.

Step 5. Place strip on a small mat board so it is easy to turn your work as you cut around template B from QS 32 Fan-tastic. Place template B on top as shown. Cut one piece at a time. Cut a total of seven fan blades.

Step 6. Arrange fan blades in order they were cut and sew them together with a scant 1/4" (menu E-1 quilt stitch on Husqvarna Viking Designers) seam allowance. Because this is sheer fabric, it looks best to press seam allowance to one side.

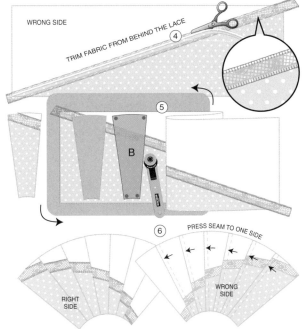

Step 7. Entredeux is used to go between two things for strength and beauty. Right sides together, place entredeux along edge of fan. Put flange of edge joining foot along raised edge of entredeux and stitch with a straight stitch. Trim seam allowance to 1/8".

Step 8. Next with the A Foot, zig zag over seam allowance (1.5 length and 3.5 width) to finish edge. Press entredeux up.

Step 9. Trim batiste (waste) from other edge of entredeux.

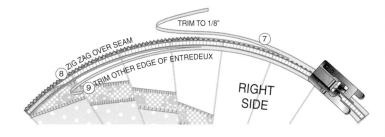

Step 10. Cut 15" of edging lace and pull header thread to slightly gather lace making it easier to shape lace along curve of fan.

Step 11. Butt straight edge of edging lace up to trimmed edge of entredeux. Place flange of edge joining foot between lace and entredeux. Zig zag with stitch length 1.5 and stitch width 2.5. The zig zag stitch goes into hole of entredeux on one side and over header of edging lace on other side.

Step 12. Place fan on point on top of a 12" square of white cotton batiste. Baste fan onto block with small zig zag stitch between lace and entredeux.

Step 13. Cut five different lengths (6", 5", 4", 3", 2") of edging lace. Pull header thread of lace to slightly gather for easy shaping. Place scalloped edge of lace over bottom point of fan block. Set machine for a lightning stitch (menu A, stitch 5) or small zig zag and sew along scalloped edge. Overlap second row of lace and repeat until the corner is filled with lace. Leave fabric behind lace for strength.

Step 14. Place fan on point on center of 16" x 10" piece of batiste. Overlap insertion lace 1/4" from straight edge of fan. Baste with small zig zag (1.5 length and 1.5 width) stitch. Baste only along inside edge of lace. Lift lace and trim excess fabric next to zig zag. Repeat on other side of fan. After excess has been removed, baste along outside edge of lace. Use a 110 universal needle to do pin stitch (menu D, stitch 46 on Husqvarna Viking Designers) over the zig zag. Trim fan block to 15" x 8 1/4".

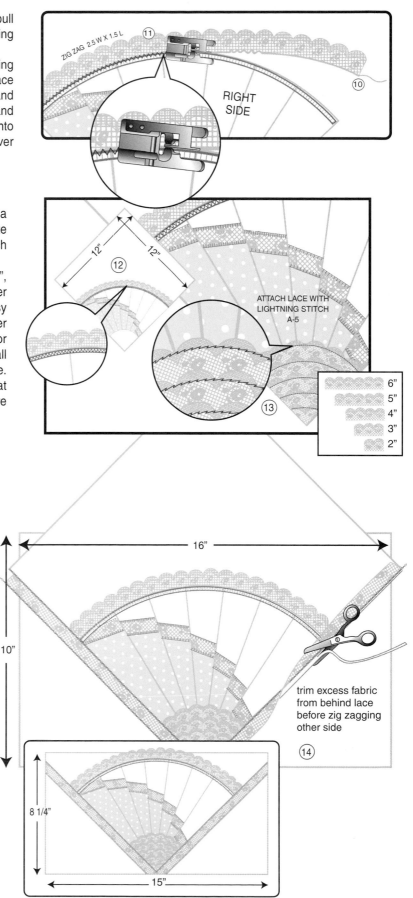

BASKET BLOCK

1 1/3 yd. insertion lace
3/4 yd. edging lace

Step 1. With water soluble marking pen trace basket pattern onto a white cotton batiste 16" x 10" rectangle. Find pattern on page 41. Using an A foot and small zig zag stitch (1.5 length and 1.5 width), center insertion lace over handle line, then baste insertion lace along outside header to form basket handle. The outside edge of lace has a shorter seam than inside edge (see diagram). Inside edge of lace will be wavy.

Step 2. Pull header thread from both ends to make handle lie flat. Lightly mist with starch and press with iron to make it lie flatter.

Step 3. Baste inside edge of handle with zig zag stitch (1.5 length and 1.5 width).

Step 4. Attach Open Toe foot. Change to a 110 universal needle and 60 wt. cotton thread. Stitch along both edges of basket handle with pin stitch (on Husqvarna Viking Designers use menu D, stitch 46) 2.5 length and 2.0 width.

Step 5. Change to a # 90 universal needle. Set machine for feather stitch (3.0 length and 6.0 width). (It is menu D, stitch 15 on Husqvarna Viking Designers.) Thread both top and bobbin with Sulky 12 wt. ecru thread. Cut four pieces of insertion lace 7" long.

Step 6. Place two pieces of insertion lace on top of Romeo Stabilizer about 1/4" apart from one another. Sew feather stitch between the two. **Note! Make sure you catch edges of both.** Repeat for the next two pieces.

Step 7. Trim away as much stabilizer as possible and soak in water until clean. Starch and press well.

Step 8. Change to #80 universal needle and 60 wt. cotton thread on top and bobbin. Place insertion panel inside basket shape and stitch with small zig zag on pattern line (1.5 length and 1.5 width).

Step 9. Starting at corner, shape edging lace around basket. Zig zag on header edge of lace with a small zig zag. Lift edging lace to remove excess of insertion panel between edge lace and fabric. Now fold fabric away from miter and sew lightning stitch or small zig zag. Trim lace tab away from miters.

Step 10. Place a Tear Away Light Stabilizer under block. Change to Sulky rayon thread. Snap on gimp foot. Snap gimp into gimp foot and gimp over header of edge lace. Set machine for small satin stitch (menu A, stitch 27 on Husqvarna Viking Designers) L-.03 W-2.0 .

Step 11. Embroider design (heirloom disk 11 design 18) over handle using ecru Sulky® rayon. Make sure to use stabilizer under embroidery. Trim block to 15" x 8 1/4".

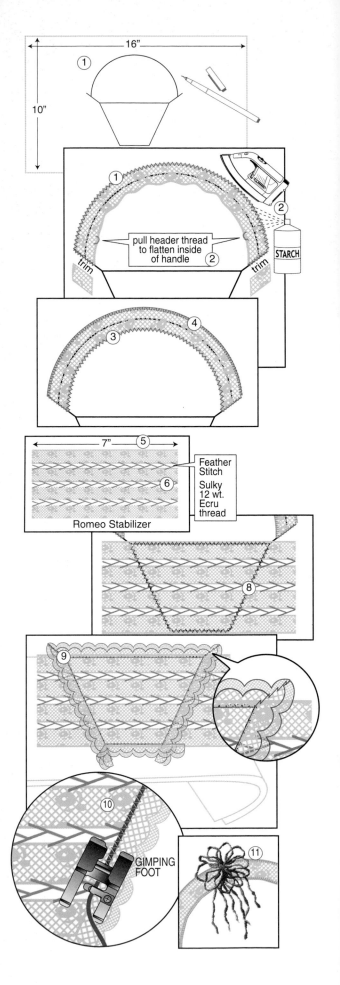

PUFFING

Puffing is quick and easy. Cut two strips of white Swiss 4 1/2" x width of fabric or 4 1/2" x 45". Cut one strip in half the long way. Sew these pieces together with wide strip in the center so seam doesn't end up in the center.

Do not speed up and slow down when sewing, but instead sew consistently same speed. If this is the first time you have done puffing, slow down speed on your machine if you have the option.

Step 1. Attach gathering foot to machine. Sew 5/8" from edge. Connie set stitch length at 4.0. The higher the stitch length the fuller the ruffle. This is a free-heirloom trim.

Step 2. Sew from top to bottom on first side and from bottom to top on second side. Don't apply pressure to fabric but gently feed at a consistent speed.

Step 3. To straighten gathers of puffing, gently stretch by holding edges of strip across from each other.

ADDING PUFFING TO TOP SECTION

Step 1. Cut a piece of batiste 13" long x 30" wide. With water soluble marking pen make a line 3/4" from bottom edge. Make a second line 3 3/4" from bottom. Add arc in center using actual size template on page 42.

Step 2. Start in center first, pinning puffing to red line along top edge. Pin at corner and continue to outside edge.

First, pin corners of bottom section, making sure gathers go straight up and down. Make adjustments with puffing as you pin along bottom edge so all gathers are straight up and down.

Step 3. Turn piece over to wrong side and zig zag (1.5 length and 1.5 width) on both red lines of template. Trim puffing seam allowance to 1/4". Shape insertion lace over both edges of puffing. Pull header threads to remove fullness on inside curves. Baste along both edges of insertion lace on **top** insertion with small zig zag.

Baste only along top edge of **bottom** insertion lace.

Step 4. Remove fabric from bottom insertion half width of lace. Use 110 universal needle and open toe foot to sew pin stitch (menu D, stitch 46) along these three edges of lace.

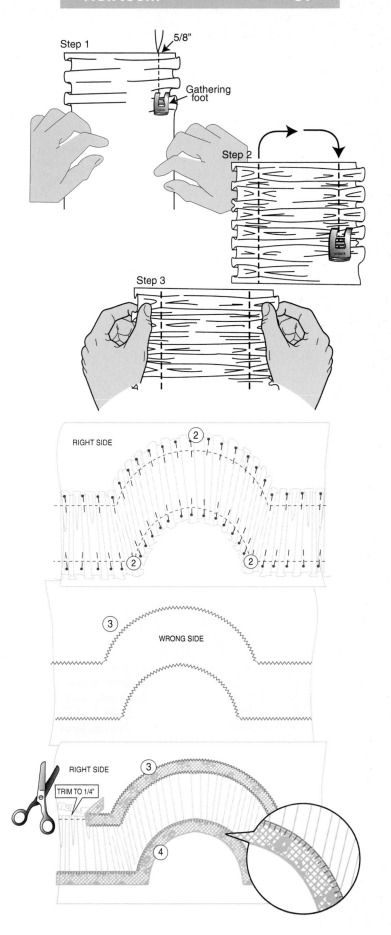

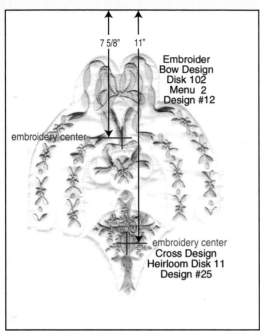

7 5/8"   11"

Embroider
Bow Design
Disk 102
Menu 2
Design #12

embroidery center

embroidery center
Cross Design
Heirloom Disk 11
Design #25

CENTER PANEL WITH EMBROIDERY

Cut a piece of batiste 16" x 15". Put tear-away light stabilizer under batiste. Embroider bow design (disk 102, menu 2. design #12) 7 5/8" from top and cross design (heirloom disk 11, design 25) 11" from top with contrasting thread. Connie used Palace Script 12 mm for her granddaughter's name. See page 30.

CONNECTING UNITS INTO ROWS

Right sides together, sew units in section two and section three together with 1/4" seam allowance. Press seam to one side. Trim seam allowance to 1/8". Baste insertion lace over center of seam with small zig zag. Use 110 universal needle and sew pin stitch (menu D, stitch 46) along both edges of lace. With a pocket scissor, trim fabric from behind lace next to pin stitch.

CONNECTING THE ROWS

Center section one over top of embroidery of section two. Pin to hold in place. Make adjustments with header thread of insertion lace on inside curve so it lies flat. Lightly mist with starch. Press. Baste with small zig zag. Next, sew along this edge with pin stitch, L-2.5 W-2.0 (menu D, stitch 46). Remove excess fabric from behind lace right next to pin stitch.

Repeat and continue connecting bottom sections with same process.

Trim quilt top to 28" x 37". For added strength place on top of another piece of white cotton batiste 40" x 49". Pin to hold in place. Overlap insertion lace 1/4" from edge of all four sides of quilt top (see photo on page 30). Baste with small zig zag only along inside edge. Fold lace to make a miter in each corner. Pin stitch over zig zag. Trim excess from between lace and top next to pin stitch.

Baste outside edge of lace and repeat with the pin stitch.

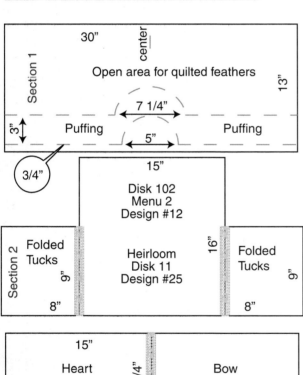

Section 1

30"   center

Open area for quilted feathers

13"

3"   Puffing   7 1/4"   Puffing
                         5"

3/4"

15"

Disk 102
Menu 2
Design #12

Heirloom
Disk 11
Design #25

Section 2   Folded   16"   Folded
             Tucks   Tucks
             9"   9"
             8"   8"

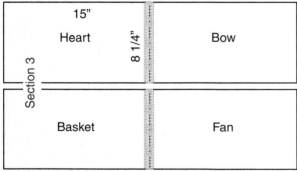

15"

Section 3   Heart   8 1/4"   Bow

             Basket   Fan

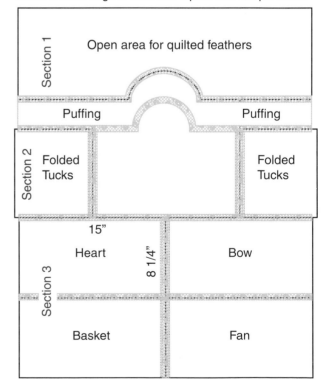

Section 1   Open area for quilted feathers

Puffing   Puffing

Section 2   Folded   Folded
             Tucks   Tucks

15"

Section 3   Heart   8 1/4"   Bow

             Basket   Fan

MADEIRA APPLIQUE BORDER

Making Madeira applique borders is easy to do with the wash-away basting thread. I speak from experience-remove this thread after finishing basting the applique so you don't use this thread by mistake for other sewing. Store this thread in a baggie so humidity doesn't get to it.

Step 1. Cut two strips of border fabric 48" x 4" for top and bottom of quilt and two strips 57" x 4" for both sides of quilt.

Step 2. Cut one strip of "America Sews Fuse and Tear" stabilizer 50" x 4" and one strip 59" x 4" Use the mini scallop radial rule to make the reusable template.

Draw a guide line 1/2" from border edge of stabilizer with a water erasable pen.

Find center of Fuse and Tear stabilizer. Start marking in the center. Place scallop ruler on top of stabilizer lining up 5" mark on ruler with the guide line. Connie used the shallow scallop. Cut stabilizer on scalloped line.

Step 3. Put two border strips right sides together. Put shiny side of stabilizer next to wrong side of border strip and press to hold in place.

Sew next to scalloped edge with water soluble thread in the bobbin. Trim to 1/4" seam allowance.

Step 4. Remove template. Trim points and clip curves close to stitching. Use a point turner to turn points of borders. Press.

Step 5. Spray starch along the seam line. Let spray absorb a couple minutes to dissolve the thread. Press until dry. Pull madeira apart. and you will have two borders exactly the same. The edge of the scallop has been turned to the inside and it is ready to apply to the outside quilt.

ATTACH MADEIRA TO QUILT EDGE

Remove water soluble thread from machine and rethread with 60 wt. cotton sewing thread.

Find center of all four sides of quilt. Put wrong side of madeira next to right side of quilt. Match center of madeira to center of quilt edge and pin to hold in place.

Fold under the corners to make a perfect miter and finger press a diagonal crease. Take borders of quilt with right sides together and sew a miter in each corner. Trim seam allowance to 1/4" and press open.

Place madeira frame on quilt and pin to hold in place. Use a 110 universal needle. Set machine for a pin stitch, L-2.5 W-1.5 (menu D, stitch 46). Sew along scallop edge with matching thread. See pages 7, 8, and 9 for instructions on how to finish your quilt.

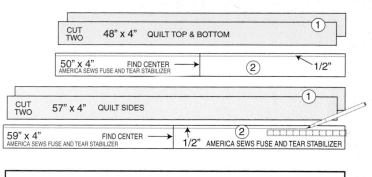

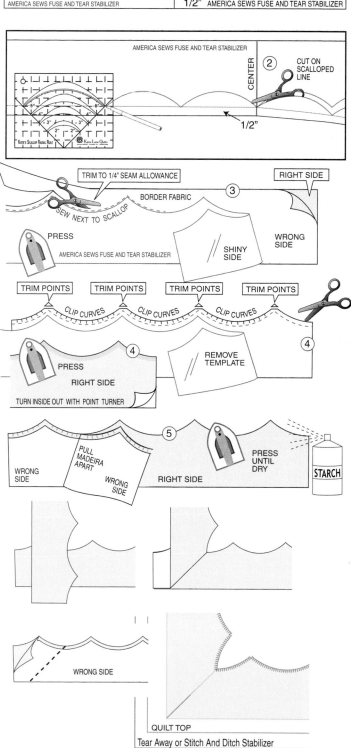

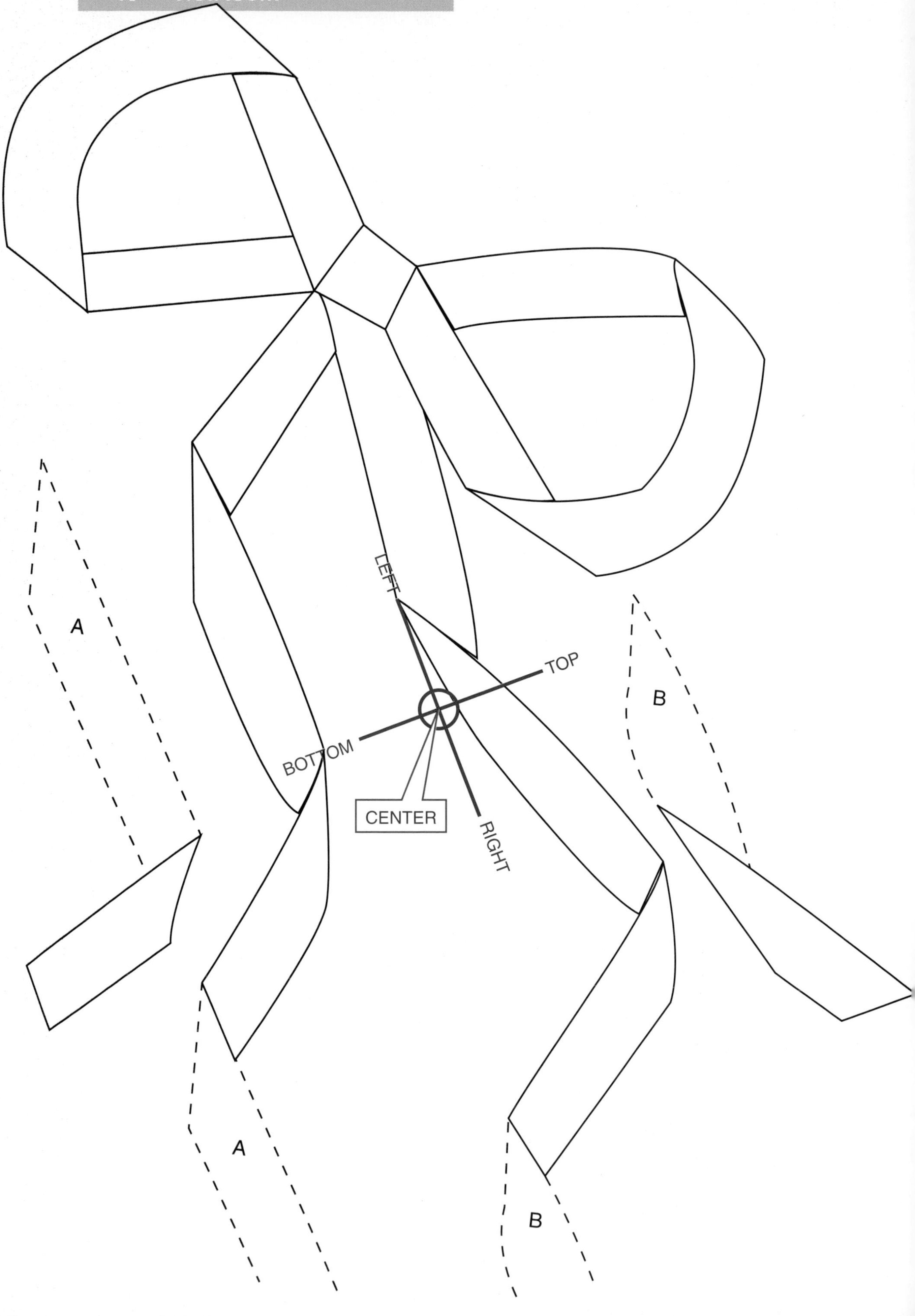

LEFT

TOP

BOTTOM

CENTER

RIGHT

A

B

A

B

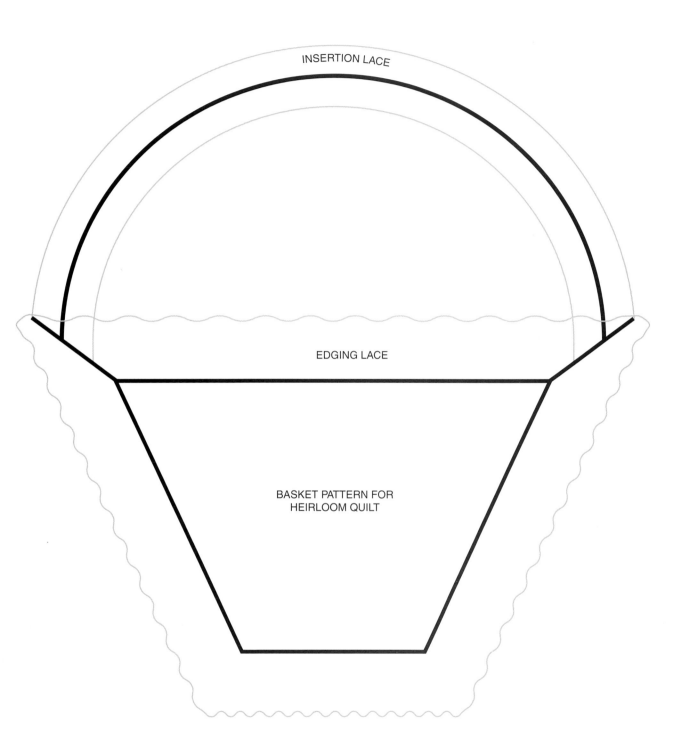

INSERTION LACE

EDGING LACE

BASKET PATTERN FOR
HEIRLOOM QUILT

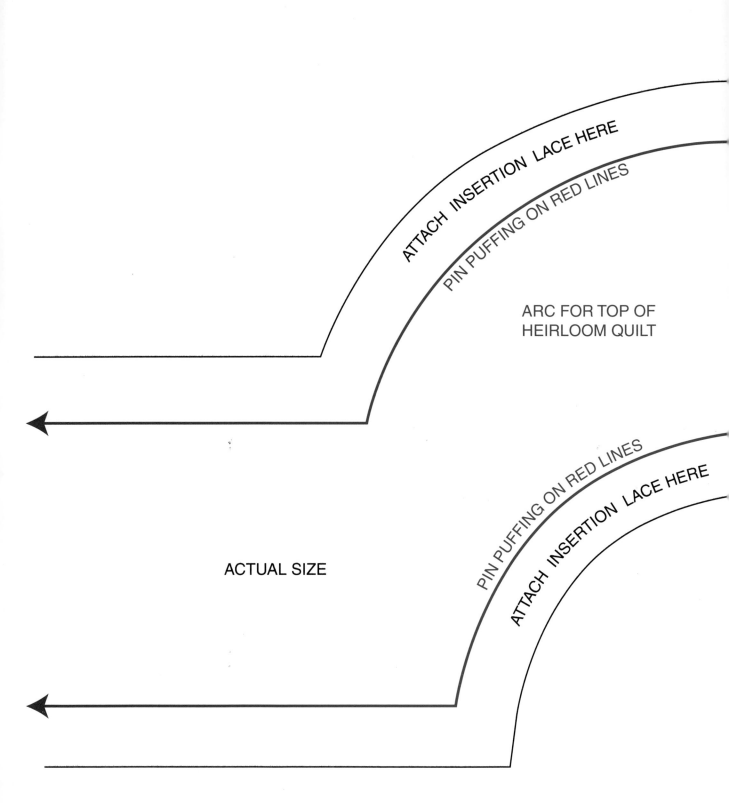

ATTACH INSERTION LACE HERE

PIN PUFFING ON RED LINES

ARC FOR TOP OF
HEIRLOOM QUILT

PIN PUFFING ON RED LINES

ATTACH INSERTION LACE HERE

ACTUAL SIZE

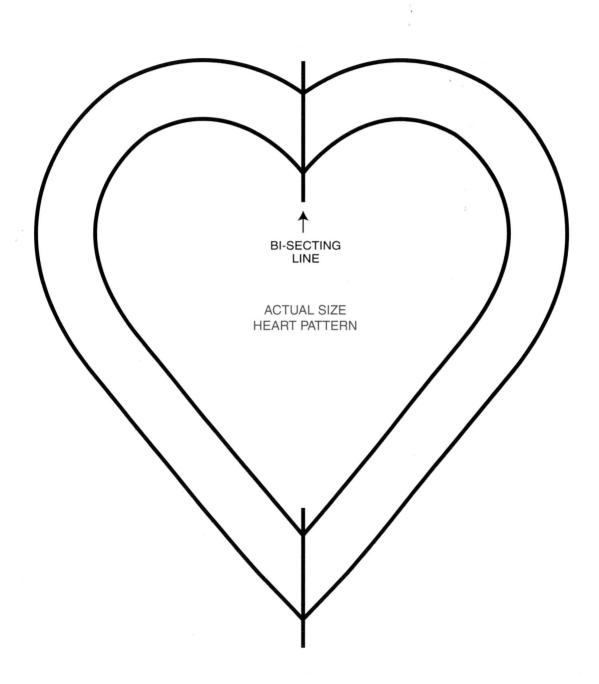

BI-SECTING
LINE

ACTUAL SIZE
HEART PATTERN

designed and made by
Patsy Shields

I
INTERMEDIATE

Ribbon Embroidery by Machine

SHOPPING LIST

4 mm. and or 7 mm. silk ribbon in the following colors:
    pink, rose, yellow, green for stems
Sulky invisible thread
Extra bobbins
Trolley needle (slips onto index finger and acts as an extension;
    thus leaving your hands free to guide the ribbon).
6" round wood machine embroidery hoop (1/4" wide)
Fade away fabric marking pencil
Size 80 (12) needle
Sulky Totally Stable iron-on stabilizer
Open-toe applique presser foot
Snag-Nabbit tool

MACHINE SET-UP FOR VINES

Step 1. On your machine, slowly wind 3 to 5 yds. 4mm. ribbon onto a bobbin. Place bobbin in bobbin case; bypass the bobbin tension and feed ribbon up through the throat plate. You can bring the ribbon up by turning the hand wheel and tugging on the needle thread to bring up the ribbon. Lengthen the stitch length to about 4.0. Put invisible thread in the needle.

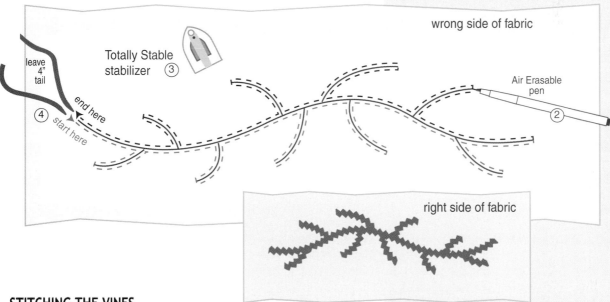

leave 4" tail

Totally Stable stabilizer ③

wrong side of fabric

Air Erasable pen ②

④ end here
start here

right side of fabric

STITCHING THE VINES

Step 2. Use the air erasable pen to draw the vines onto the fabric you want to embellish. You will only need a faint outline. This is your stitching guide.

Step 3. Keep in mind the area you wish to embellish. Iron a piece of Totally Stable stabilizer on the wrong side of the fabric or garment using a dry iron.

Step 4. Place the open-toe applique presser foot on the machine and slowly begin to stitch on the wrong side of the garment or fabric. The open-toe foot has a tunnel on the bottom which makes it easier to feed fabric when there is a build up. If you stitch down the vine and back again it will give you a fuller vine shape and you will not have to cut the ribbon. Just stitch down, raise the presser foot with needle down in the fabric, turn and stitch beside the first stitching (not on top of it for a fuller looking leaf). Continue in this manner until you reach the end of the vine pattern.

Raise the presser foot, grab the fabric holding onto the ribbon underneath and carefully pull it from the sewing area. Be sure to leave about a 4" tail of ribbon at the beginning and end of the vine; use the Snag Nabbit or tapestry needle to feed the tails to the back of the work and secure. See illustration. Carefully remove the stabilizer.

Step 5. Place fabric in a wooden machine embroidery hoop right side up (as shown on page 44). Remove presser foot, insert a bobbin of invisible thread in the bobbin case and lower the feed dogs. Now you can begin making the flowers on and beside the vine until you have a full flower arrangement.

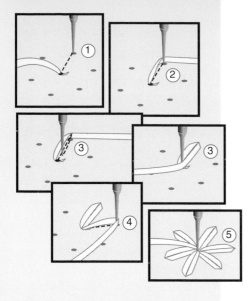

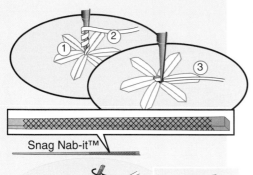

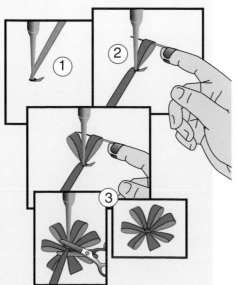

Snag Nab-it™

DAISIES

Step 1. With a fade-away marker, make a dot for the center of the flower and 5 dots around the outside. Cut a length of ribbon about 12" long. Tack one end of the ribbon on the center dot. Hold the ribbon to the back out of the way and stitch out to the first dot.

Step 2. Stop with the needle down in the fabric. Bring the ribbon around the needle (ribbon should stand at the back of the needle). Leave a little slack in ribbon so it will have a curve. Take a single stitch backward over the ribbon to make it lie down.

Step 3. Move the ribbon away from the needle and stitch back to the center on the right side of the petal. Let the ribbon lie flat on the fabric so it looks like the left side. Pull the ribbon against the needle and stitch it down at the center.

Step 4. Stitch out to the next dot. Repeat the previous step, always coming back to the center. Continue until all petals are finished.

Step 5. Stitch back and forth over the ribbon before cutting off the ends close to the stitching.

FRENCH KNOTS

Fill the center with French knots. You can use the same color and you would make them before cutting off the ribbon tails or you can tack another color of ribbon in the center and make knots. You can also make individual leaves this way.

Step 1. Tack the tail of the ribbon where you want the knots to be - in the center of a flower or just a cluster of knots.

Step 2. Stop with the needle down in the fabric and wrap the ribbon about three times around the needle. Loosen the ribbon slightly so you can turn the hand wheel to bring the needle out of the ribbon.

Step 3. Place the needle back in the fabric beside the ribbon and a little knot will form. Make one or more in the center of flowers. You can also make bullion roses by wrapping the ribbon 6 times around the needle. Raise the needle up, move out the width of the ribbon. Lay it down and stitch in place to secure.

Step 4. Use Snag Nabbit to pull tails to back.

LOOP FLOWER

Step 1. Put a dot where you want the center of the flower. Use a 7mm. pink ribbon about 9" long. Tack the end of pink ribbon in the center of flower.

Step 2. Place a trolley needle on your index finger, loop the ribbon over it and bring the ribbon back to the starting point. Tack it down.

Step 3. Slightly rotate the hoop. To make a second loop the same length as the first one, slip the trolley needle into the first loop. Tack the second loop down. All sewing is done in the center of the flower.

When all the loops are done, tack the ribbon securely and cut off the ribbon close to the stitching. You can also make a French knot at the bottom.

ROSE

Step 1. Make three dots 1/4" apart in a triangle to mark the center of the rose. Use 4mm. ribbon for a tiny rose and 7 mm. for a larger rose. Cut ribbon about 12" long.

Step 2. Remove presser foot. Insert the needle into one of the dots and take a few stitches. Find center of ribbon by folding it in half. Give it a twist and push the twist up against the needle. Tack it in place.

Step 3. Stitch to the next dot.

Step 4. Cross the ribbon in front of the needle (left over right).

Step 5. Jump over the ribbon with the needle and make one tack stitch.

Step 6. Rotate the hoop. Stitch to next dot. Cross ribbon in front of needle (left over right). Repeat step 5 and tack in place.

Step 7. Stitch back to the starting point to complete the center of the flower (bud).

Step 8. To make the outer flower petals, stitch 1/8" from edge of flower going around the center bud. Stitch 1/2" and cross over ribbon in front of needle. Continue until the flower is the size you want.

Step 9. Hide the ribbon ends under the flower. Hold in place with a stiletto and stitch to hold in place. Cut tails.

You can use these techniques to embellish evening bags, garments, picture frames, and much more.

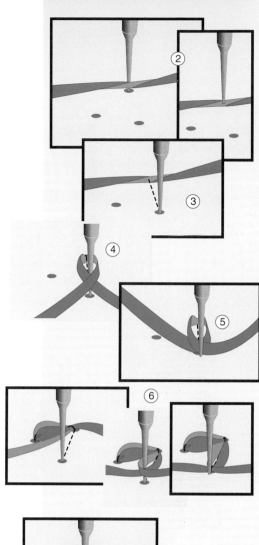

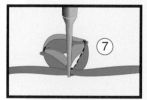

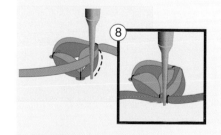

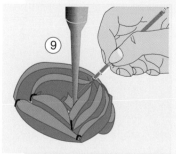

Storm At Sea Yardage
54" x 54"

3/8 yd. lightest blue		1/2 yd.	
5/8 Yd. dark blue		5/8 Yd.	
3/8 yd. printed blue		1 1/2 yd. outside border	
3/4 yd. inside border/binding		3 yds. backing	

designed, pieced,
& quilted by
Sharlene Jorgenson

INTERMEDIATE

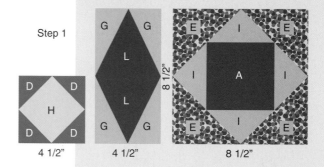

Step 1

SHOPPING LIST
Sp1 Peaky and Spike templates
Fabric Grips
Large and small mat board
6" x 24" Omnigrid® ruler
Glass head silk pins 0.05 mm
Stiletto
Flannel board
17" x 17" Q Snap frame
Open toe foot 412 27 70-45
Low-loft batting

ABOUT STORM AT SEA

Step 1. The combination of weird angles creates the illusion of curves in this quilt. The square on point, diamond and square in a square are the only units needed to make the quilt. You can use three, four or five fabrics to make the Storm at Sea pattern. I used two golds with different texture but the same value. The three blues with different value and texture added so much to the design.

I suggest making copies of page 55 so you can color your own design.

CUTTING INSTRUCTIONS
Use templates D, H, A, E, G, L, and I to make Storm At Sea.

Step 2. To straighten fabric see page 4.
Cut three strips 2 7/8" wide for template D.
Cut three strips 3 3/4" wide for template I.
Cut two strips 4 7/8" wide for template E.

Place strips the same width on top of each other making sure edges line are in line. Bifold strips on a small mat board so it is easier to turn your work as you cut around the template. Flip-flop template cutting pieces as you go. The bias edge is always on the long edge of each piece and straight of grain is on both short edges. See diagram for number of pieces to cut.

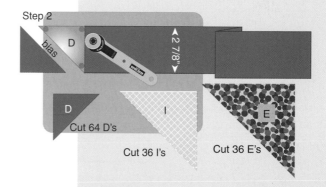

Step 2

Cut 64 D's

Cut 36 I's

Cut 36 E's

Step 3. Cut 4 strips 4 1/2" wide for template G.
Fold strip in half so you end with a right G and left G (mirror image) each time you cut around the G template. Remove selvage edges before cutting pieces. See diagram for number of G's to cut.

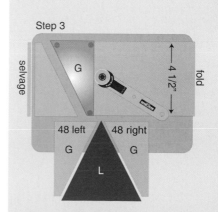

Step 3

48 left   48 right

Step 4

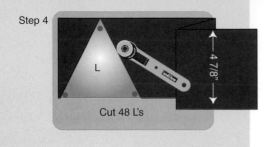

Cut 48 L's

Step 4. Cut three strips 4 7/8" wide for template L. Place strips on top of each other making sure edges are in line. Bifold strips on a small mat board so it is easier to turn your work as you cut around the template. Flip-flop template cutting pieces as you go. The long sides are on the bias and the short edge is on the straight of grain. See diagram for number of pieces to cut.

Step 5

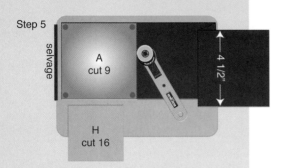

selvage

A
cut 9

4 1/2"

H
cut 16

Step 5. Cut one strip 4 1/2" wide for template A. Cut two strips 3 3/8" wide for template H. Place strips on top of each other. Make sure edges are lined up before cutting. Remove selvage edge. See diagram for number of pieces to cut.

SEWING INSTRUCTIONS

Step 6a. Sew all seams with a scant 1/4" seam allowance. (Menu A stitch 1 on Husqvarna Viking Designers.)

Right sides together, center bias edge of D on top of H. Ears should hang out evenly. Notice seam does not start in crevice. You should see a couple stitches on the triangle before hitting the square. I make the first stitches on an anchor cloth so beginning stitches on patchwork are as strong as center stitches sewn. Guide pieces in front of presser foot with stiletto to prevent pieces from scooting to one side at end of seam. Do not back stitch at beginning or end of seam.

b. Finger press seam open before pressing with an iron. It works much better to finger press on a hard surface before going to the ironing board. There is too much cushion on the ironing board and you risk the chance of getting pleats in the seam well.

c. Center second D on opposite edge of H. Sew seam.

d. Finger press seam open.

e. Attach D triangles to opposite edges of unit. The mouse ears will hang out evenly. This time seam will begin and end in the crevice. Do not back stitch.

f. You will know it is right when edges are straight and points are 1/4" from edge. Place template A (4 1/2" square) on top and trim off ears with rotary cutter. If you are a beginner and your seam allowance is too scant, extra fabric can be removed with second method.

Make sixteen of these units.

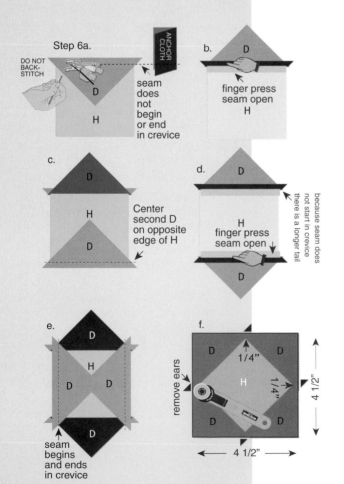

SQUARE IN A SQUARE

Step 7a. Follow step 6a through 6f when making the first part of this square in a square. Put an A square on point in the center surrounded by four I's.

b. Right sides together, center bias edge of E on bottom of unit. Ears should hang out evenly. It is best to sew this seam with E on the bottom so intersection you want to sew over is visible. This gives you a perfect point on the right side. Notice seam does not start in crevice. You should see a couple stitches on the triangle before hitting the square. I make the first stitches on an anchor cloth so beginning stitches on patchwork are as strong as center stitches sewn. Guide pieces in front of presser foot with stiletto to prevent pieces from scooting to one side at end of seam. Do not back stitch at beginning or end of seam.

c. Add the second E to opposite edge. Finger press seams open before pressing with an iron. It works much better to finger press on a hard surface before going to the ironing board. There is too much cushion on the ironing board and you risk the chance of getting pleats in the seam well.

d. Attach E triangle to third edge of unit. The mouse ears will hang out evenly. This time seam will begin and end in the crevice. Do not back stitch.

e. Add the second E to opposite edge. Press seam open.

f. You will know it is right when the edges are straight. This block should measure 8 1/2". Make nine of these units.

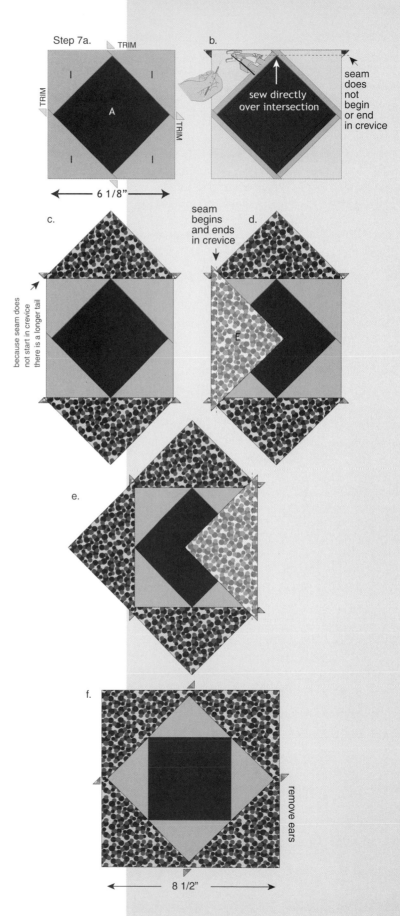

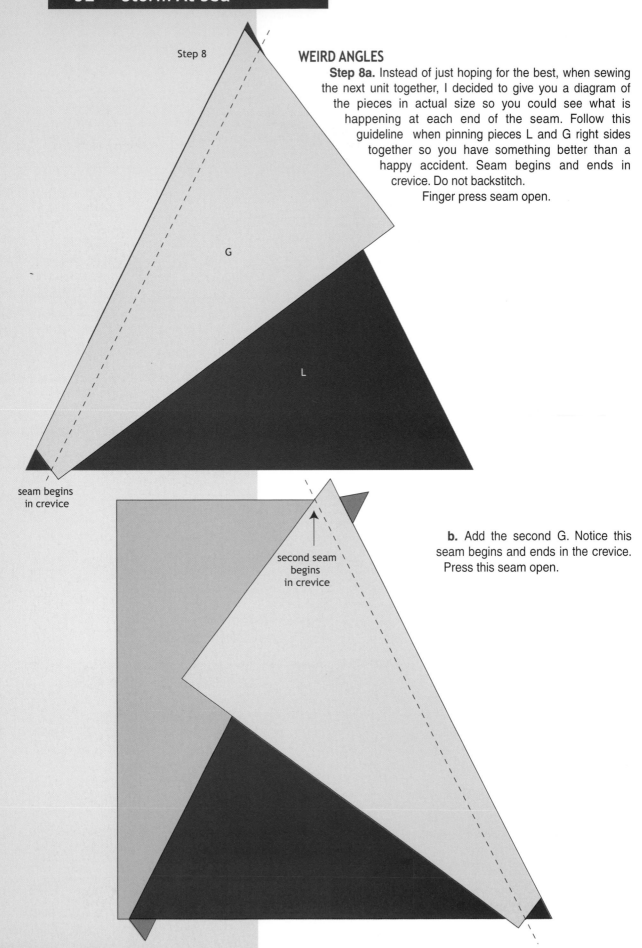

Step 8

G

L

seam begins
in crevice

WEIRD ANGLES

Step 8a. Instead of just hoping for the best, when sewing the next unit together, I decided to give you a diagram of the pieces in actual size so you could see what is happening at each end of the seam. Follow this guideline when pinning pieces L and G right sides together so you have something better than a happy accident. Seam begins and ends in crevice. Do not backstitch.

Finger press seam open.

second seam
begins
in crevice

b. Add the second G. Notice this seam begins and ends in the crevice. Press this seam open.

Step 9a. Place unit (made in step 8) on top of a small mat board. Put template A on top of sewn unit. Trim off ears with a rotary cutter. You should have a 4 1/2" square.

Make 48 of these units.

b. Right sides together, put two of these units together. Make sure they are turned in the right direction to form a diamond when sewn. To make a perfect intersection, insert a pin 1/4" from edge on the seam line through top and bottom. Leave this pin standing.

c. Insert another pin at an angle as shown and remove the standing pin. Do not back stitch at beginning or end of seam. Finger press seam open before pressing with an iron. The intersections should be 1/4" from the edge.

d. This unit should measure 8 1/2" x 4 1/2". Make 24 of these units.

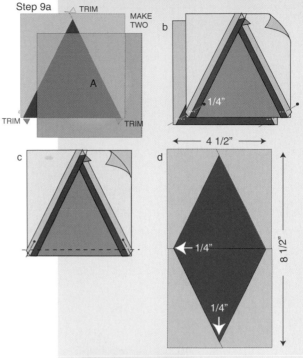

Step 10. Arrange units into rows as shown in step 11. Put units right sides together. Insert a pin through top and bottom intersection 1/4" from the edge. Leave this pin standing. Insert another pin on each side of standing pin and sew seam. Press seam open.

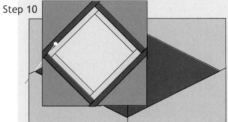

Step 11. Continue to sew all rows together. Connect the rows.

One block would make a nice pillow and a row would make a nice table runner.

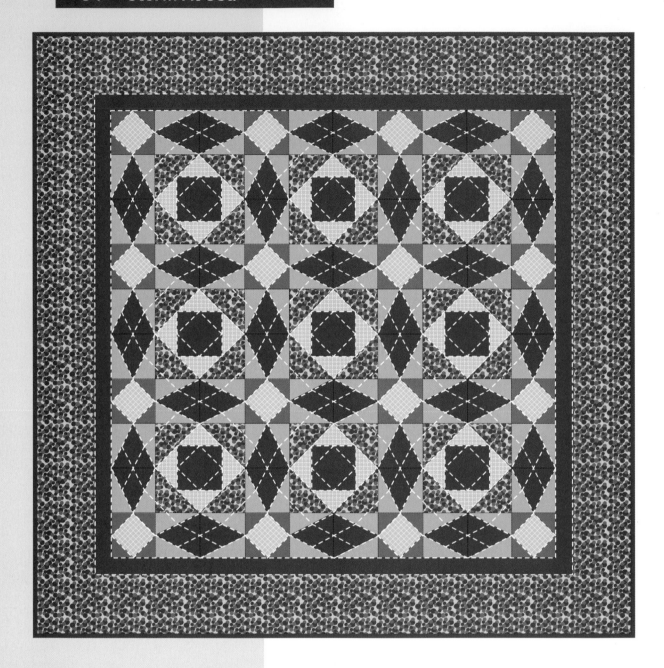

Step 12. Cut the strips for outside border 6" wide and inside border strips are 2" wide. To add mitered borders see page 7. To make quilt sandwich see page 8; binding instructions are on page 9.

FINISHING TOUCHES

The white dashed line indicates the way my "Storm At Sea" was quilted. Meandering was done in the border.

designed and made by McKenna Ryan

Moon Over Montana Yardage *finished size 21"w x 22"h*

PALE BLUE	SKY BACKGROUND	13 3/4" x 14 3/4"
PURPLE (MEDIUM)	INNER BORDER & BINDING	1/4 yd
PURPLE (DARK)	OUTER BORDER	1/4 yd
PURPLE (MULTI-SHADED)	HUCKLEBERRIES	6" SQUARE
GREEN (LIGHTEST)	TWO HUCKLEBERRY BRANCHES	12 1/2" W X 6"H
GREEN (LIGHT)	**A** EVERGREEN TREE	4 1/2" W X 6 1/2"H
GREEN (MEDIUM)	**B** EVERGREEN TREE	5 1/4"W X 8"H
GREEN (DARK)	GRASS	14"W X 3 1/4"
GREEN (DARKEST)	**C** EVERGREEN TREE	7" W X 9"H
WHITE	MOON	2 3/4" SQUARE
TAN	BEAR SNOUTS	1 1/2" SQUARE
BROWN (LIGHT)	**A** BEAR	3"W X 3 3/4"H
BROWN (MEDIUM)	**B** BEAR	2 3/4"W X 3 1/2"H
BROWN (DARK)	**C** BEAR	2 3/4"W X 5 1/4"H
BROWN (DARKEST)	TREE	5"W X 12"H

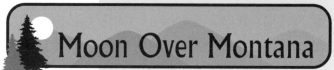

SHOPPING LIST
Fabric marking pencil
Applique pressing sheet
Template plastic
Heat n Bond or Trans Web
Invisible monofilament thread
12 weight Sulky® thread
Open toe foot
Open Toe Stippling foot
Low-loft batting

CHOOSING FABRIC

McKenna likes to use batik fabrics because they have a high thread count. Batiks have lots of beautiful color changes and interesting textures that are fun to use when making a picture quilt. She does not wash the fabric before making her quilts.

FUSIBLE WEB APPLIQUE INSTRUCTIONS

Step 1. Trace each of the applique shapes separately on the smooth paper side of Trans Web or your favorite iron-on adhesive. Be sure to allow space between shapes so that each can be cut loosely around the tracing lines.

Step 2. Cut out each paper shape approximately 1/4" out from your drawing line.

Step 3. Study your fabric to find color changes you want to take advantage of before pressing patterns onto back side. For example, if you cut all the Huckleberries from the same area, there will be less dimension in the picture. Next, cut out each of the applique pieces following the drawing line on the paper side of fusible web.

After pieces have been fused to wrong side of fabric and cut to shape, they will be facing the same direction as seen in photo.

Step 4. In this pattern, all applique drawings are in reverse of actual finished design.

Trans Web or iron-on adhesive

wrong side

peel off

Step 5

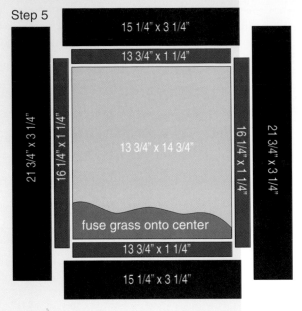

15 1/4" x 3 1/4"

13 3/4" x 1 1/4"

21 3/4" x 3 1/4"

16 1/4" x 1 1/4"

13 3/4" x 14 3/4"

16 1/4" x 1 1/4"

21 3/4" x 3 1/4"

fuse grass onto center

13 3/4" x 1 1/4"

15 1/4" x 3 1/4"

PREPARATION OF QUILT TOP

Step 5. Follow diagram and cut pieces for quilt back as shown. Peel off paper backing from grass. Align bottom and side edges of grass to sky background. Press with iron to hold in place before inside border is attached so edges on three sides are included in seam allowance.

Attach inside border to top and bottom of sky. Next attach sides. Repeat and add outside border.

Step 6. Peel off paper backing from rest of applique pieces. Place cut applique pieces with fusible side down on background piece of fabric referring to quilt photo. Remember to tuck any seam allowances behind the shape on top of it. Great tip! Tap lightly with iron over applique. Hold up to see if you like the placement. If you don't like the placement, you can lift the applique after it is cool if you didn't press too much. If you have used fabric with a high thread count, the edges won't fray when pieces are lifted to be moved. Fuse according to the manufacture's directions.

McKenna likes to think outside the border when designing her quilts. In this quilt she placed the branches and Huckleberries in upper right and lower left corners.

TUG TOP THREAD
TO POP BOBBIN THREAD
THROUGH QUILT LAYERS

See page 8 to make quilt sandwich. Cut backing and batting so that it extends 2"-3" beyond quilt top.

Read machine quilting tips on page 5 before continuing. Thread machine with monofilament thread on top and cotton thread to match back in bobbin.

Lower feed dogs. Start quilting in the center. Put your quilt under the needle and draw bottom thread up through fabric. Holding both threads, take a few stitches in one place. Cut loose threads.

Start sewing at a slow speed and move the quilt as you sew. You will feel tension between the quilt and needle. If you move the quilt too fast, you may break a needle. If you move it too slow your stitches may be too small. Now increase the speed of your machine and begin to move the quilt at a steady, even pace. You will begin to feel that you are getting a rhythm to your movements. Stitch around edges (1/8" from edge) of each applique using this free motion method of machine quilting. Use your imagination and add clouds and more detail to trees and bears if you wish.

Sew 1/4" from edge of quilt. Trim off extra fabric and bind following instructions on page 9.

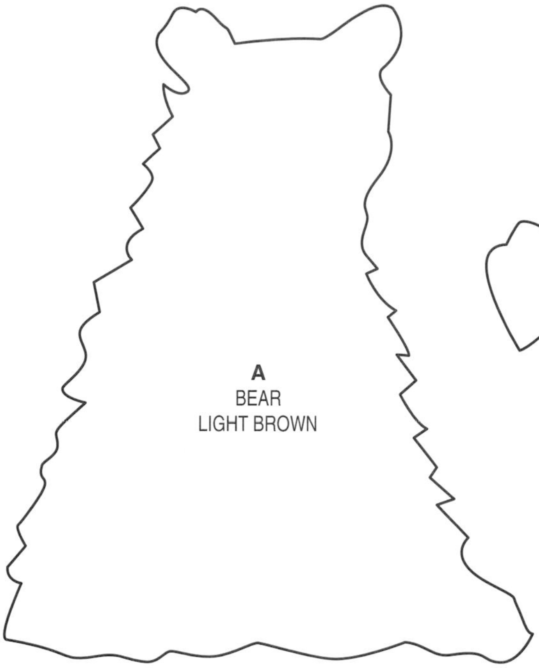

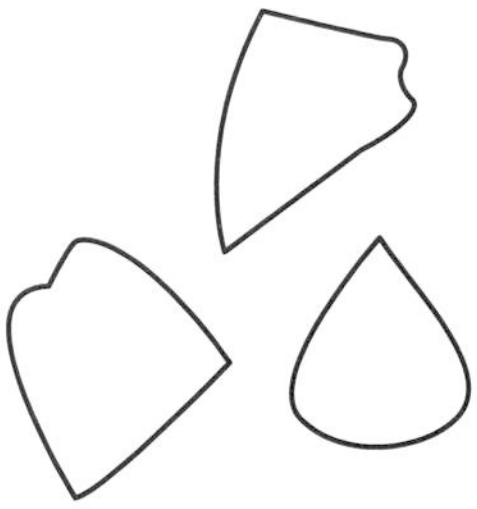

A
BEAR
LIGHT BROWN

BEAR S SNOUTS
TAN

For more Pine Needles patterns contact:

Pine Needles Designs, Inc.
P.O. Box 2379
Bigfork, Montana 59911
406-837-0423
www.pineneedles.com

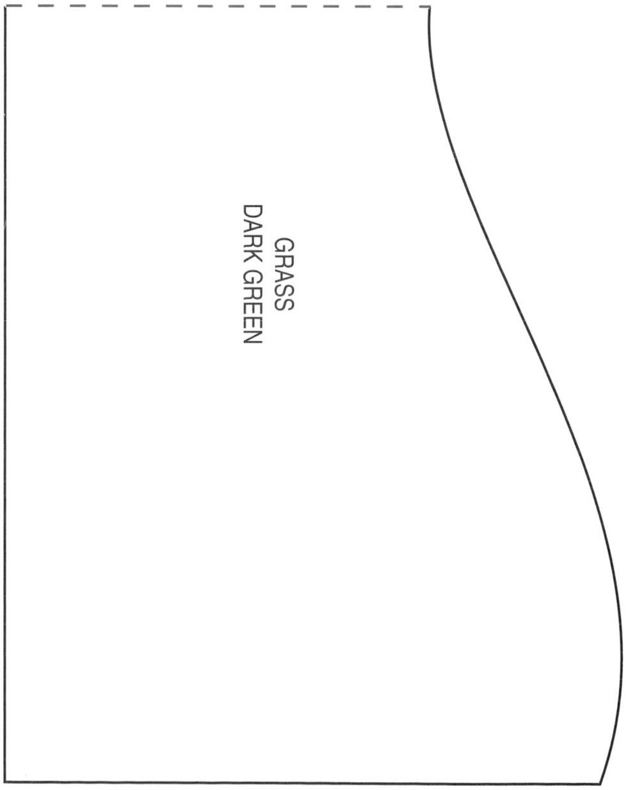

GRASS
DARK GREEN

GRASS
DARK GREEN

B
BEAR
MEDIUM BROWN

C
BEAR DARK BROWN

TREE
DARKEST BROWN

TREE
DARKEST BROWN

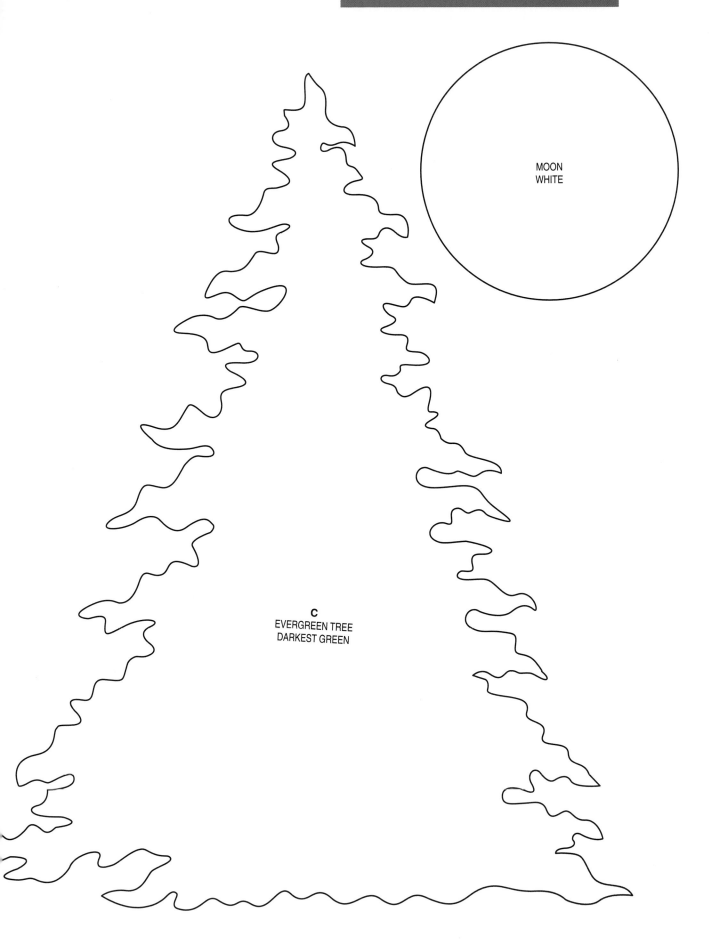

MOON
WHITE

C
EVERGREEN TREE
DARKEST GREEN

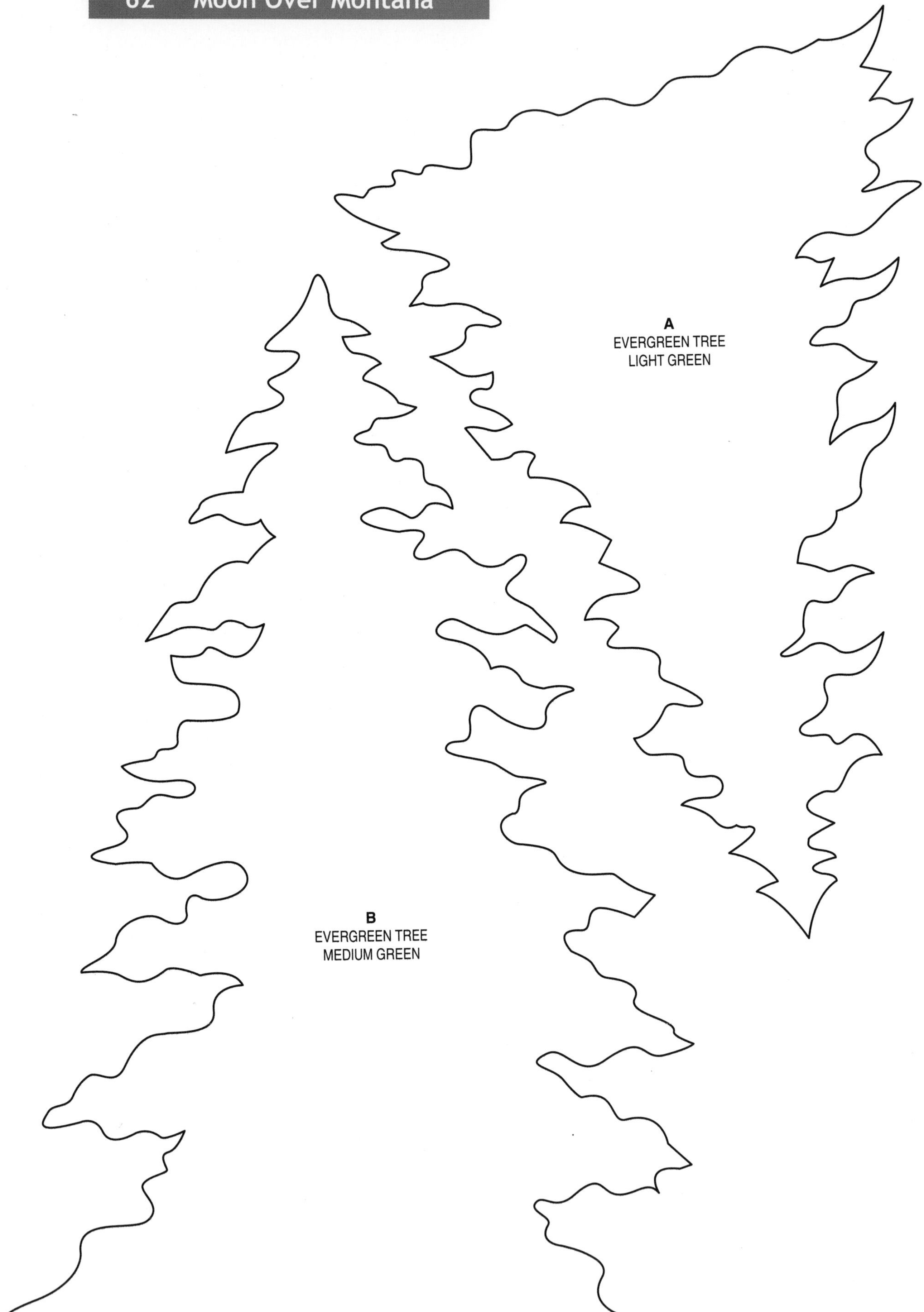

A
EVERGREEN TREE
LIGHT GREEN

B
EVERGREEN TREE
MEDIUM GREEN

HUCKLEBERRIES
MULTI-SHADED PURPLE

HUCKLEBERRY
BRANCHES
LIGHTEST GREEN

HUCKLEBERRY
BRANCHES
LIGHTEST GREEN

HUCKLEBERRIES
MULTI-SHADED PURPLE

Notes

Other books by Shar

100 SERIES

1000 SERIES

900 SERIES

800 SERIES

700 SERIES

600 SERIES

500 SERIES

300 SERIES

200 SERIES

Quilter's Companion Cookbook

3" Curved Two Patch

Double Wedding Ring

Miniature Double Wedding Ring

Add On to Double Wedding Ring

Pickle Dish & Indian Double Wedding Ring

Crazy Quilt

Miniature Crazy Quilt

Fan-Tastic

Wheel of Mystery

Grandmother's Flower Garden

Mariner's Compass

Apple Core

Heartland Log Cabin

Miniature Log Cabin

Quilter's Starter Kit

Dresden Plate

To purchase these books check your local quilt shop or call 1-800-637-2541
Look for us online at www.qheartland.com

designed by
Sharlene Jorgenson

pieced by Mickey Roy

machine quilted by
Jean Johnson

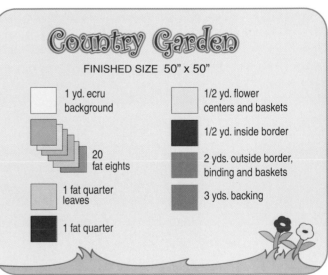

Country Garden

FINISHED SIZE 50" x 50"

1 yd. ecru
background

20
fat eights

1 fat quarter
leaves

1 fat quarter

1/2 yd. flower
centers and baskets

1/2 yd. inside border

2 yds. outside border,
binding and baskets

3 yds. backing

B
BEGINNER

COUNTRY GARDEN

Use templates A, B, C, & D from Log Cabin template set.

Reproduction prints from the thirties were used for diagonal paths and ecru for background. At each intersection there is a flower made of four red squares with a yellow center. It's important to have a high contrast between the light background and path so the design doesn't get lost.

Inside border is red and the blue used for flower pots was also used for outside border. A complementary continuous line flower and leaf design is quilted in the scalloped border.

Step 1. You only have to know how to make one block to make this quilt. After all blocks are made you twist and turn them to create the diagonal path. Blocks are separated with red squares sewn to end of a C log.

STRAIGHTEN FABRIC AND CUT STRIPS

Step 2. See page 4 to straighten fabric and cut strips.

Place six strips on top of each other and align edges. Place template A on top and cut 6 A's at a time. 50 different prints were used in the path. I suggest you use no less than 20 different prints in the path. To keep colors evenly distributed, separate pieces into piles and put into zip lock sandwich bags.

Cut 13 yellow squares and 60 red squares for flowers from template A.

Step 3. From light fabric, cut strips for logs A, B, C, and D 1 3/4" wide. Place strips on top of each other and line up edges. Place template on top of strips and cut number of logs needed (see diagram).

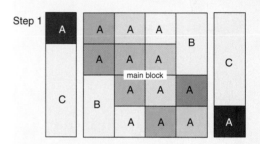

Step 1

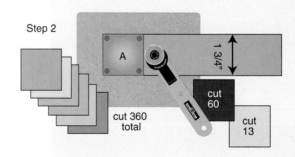

Step 2

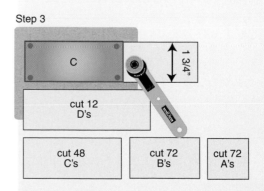

Step 3

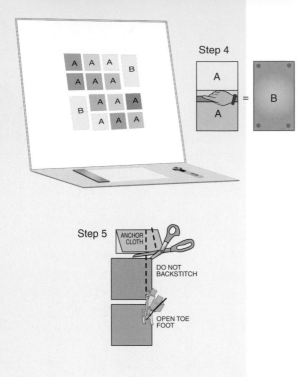

Step 4

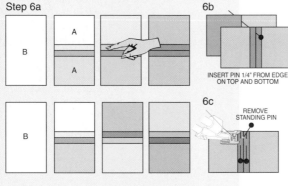

Step 5

ANCHOR CLOTH

DO NOT BACKSTITCH

OPEN TOE FOOT

Step 6a

B
A
A

6b

INSERT PIN 1/4" FROM EDGE ON TOP AND BOTTOM

6c

REMOVE STANDING PIN

B

Step 7

B

make 72

finger press seam open

3"

5 1/2"

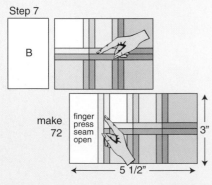

Step 8

wrong side

5 1/2"

5 1/2"

sew 36 blocks

SEWING INSTRUCTIONS

Step 4. Before starting to chain sew, give yourself a sewing test. Set sewing machine for the scant 1/4" seam allowance.

On "Designer I" touch menu E quilt stitch 1

On "Designer 2" insert Stitch D-card, touch E1

On "Quilt Designer" insert Stitch E1 card, touch 1

I prefer using an open toe foot so you have an unobstructed view when sewing. Two A's sewn together must equal the B piece. Continue, after passing sewing test.

This is a simple quilt to make but you must use the right order of construction to avoid getting confused. Arrange pieces for one block on a flannel board to make it easier to distribute color and texture evenly.

To create a path, top and bottom row should include a light A on opposite corners. A light B on opposite corners completes one block.

Step 5. Use an anchor cloth when starting to chain sew to maintain strength of beginning and ending stitches. Make sure to include two light A's for each block.

Step 6

a. It is much easier to finger press seams open on a hard surface. After units are pressed with iron, arrange them again on flannel board to prevent confusion.

b. When connecting units, insert a pin 1/4" from edge through top and bottom units.

c. Insert another pin on each side of standing pin. Remove standing pin. Do not back stitch at either end of seam because it would create bulk at intersections. When connecting units together make sure they all have the light A in upper left corner.

Step 7. Use pinning technique in steps 6b-6c when connecting the rows. Finger press seams open.

Add light B piece to end that has light A in upper left corner (on wrong side). Finger press seam open, then press with an iron.

This unit should measure 3" wide by 5 1/2" long. It is easy to check the units with a 3" x 18" Omnigrid® ruler. Make 72 units.

Step 8. Turn one unit made in step 7 180° so light B's end up in opposite corners. Sew seam. Press seams open.

Each block should be a 5 1/2" square. Every time you start a new block, shuffle pieces to distribute evenly colors and texture.

Make 36 blocks for wall quilt.

CONNECTING COUNTRY GARDEN BLOCK

Step 9. Add 48 C's and 12 D's to red A squares cut in step 2. These units create flowers at intersections between blocks. Both C and D logs are used in horizontal connecting rows. Press seams open.

Step 10. Arrange blocks completed in step 8 into rows. Twist and turn blocks as shown in diagram to create a diagonal design. Alternate direction of red A's connected to C's (made in step 9) between blocks. Put light C parallel to light side of block.

Use pinning technique in step 6 and sew seams.

Step 11. Connect rows together.

BORDERS

Step 12. Cut 4 strips for inside border 2" wide from selvage to selvage.

Attach inside border to top and bottom. Next attach inside borders to each side.

Cut 4 strips 6" wide 54" long for outside border. See page 7 if you want outside border to have miters.

APPLIQUÉ

Step 13. Trace applique patterns on page 71 onto template plastic and cut out with scissor.

Step 14. Iron "Trans Web" or "Heat n Bond" to wrong side of fabrics used for appliques.

Step 15. Place plastic template for basket on wrong side of yellow fabric. Trace 6 baskets and cut out.

Do the same for the flower pots on blue fabric and flowers and leaves on appropriate fabrics.

Remove paper backing.

Step 16. Place applique pressing sheet on top of placement pattern. Because the sheet is transparent it allows you to see your pattern to use as a placement guide while you fuse your overlapping design together into one unit. Pay attention to order (1-5) and press each piece in place on applique pressing sheet.

Step 17. When cool, gently peel off entire applique from pressing sheet. The overlapping edges of individual pieces are fused together. The sticky backing will not adhere to pressing sheet. Because the design is now all one piece, instead of several small pieces, you can easily move it around until you are satisfied with its placement. Place in center of each block as shown in quilt picture.

Step 18. Use matching 12 wt. cotton thread on top and 30 wt. cotton in the bobbin. Applique with a blanket stitch. I used menu F stitch 15 (2.5L and 2.5 W) on Husqvarna Viking.

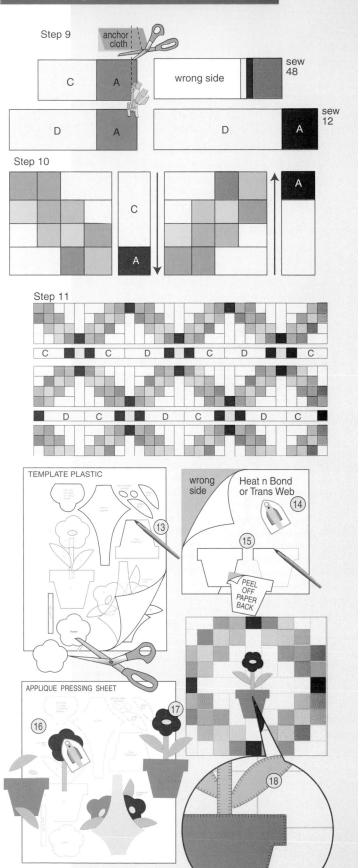

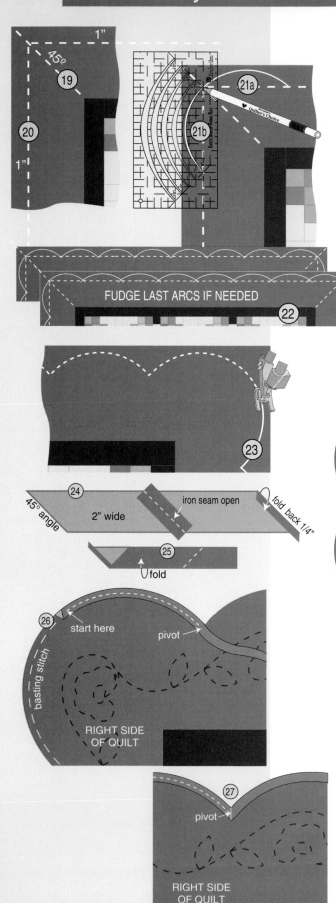

SCALLOPED EDGE ON BORDER

Step 19. Mark all four corners with 45° miter if you didn't sew mitered corners. Use 45° line on ruler as an aid.

Step 20. Draw a guide line 1" from edge of border on all four sides with water erasable pencil. Moving guide in or out changes length of guide line.

Step 21. Corners are made from two arcs (21a and 21b). Draw four corners using arc of your choice. Rotate ruler 90° to draw second arc. Repeat on all four corners.

Step 22. Fill in with more arcs between corners. Work from corners toward center to maintain symmetry. Fudge last arcs if needed to fit in remaining space.

Step 23. Stay stitch before making quilt sandwich so you have a permanent guide to go by.

See page 8 to make quilt sandwich.

QUILTING

There are three diagonal lines quilted in the dark path. Meandering was done in the light background. We made up a continuous line flower/leaf design to go in the outside border for a complementary ending.

BINDING

Step 24. Cut 2" strips on the bias. Trim both ends of all strips at a 45º angle. Sew strips together and press seams open. Fold 1/4" back at the beginning.

Step 25. Fold binding in half.

Step 26. Place binding on right side. Start sewing 1" after the 1/4" fold. Do not stretch binding as you sew. When you get to inside curve, stop with needle in down position. Lift presser foot.

Step 27. Readjust fabric and sew along edge of next curve.

Flip binding to backside of quilt.

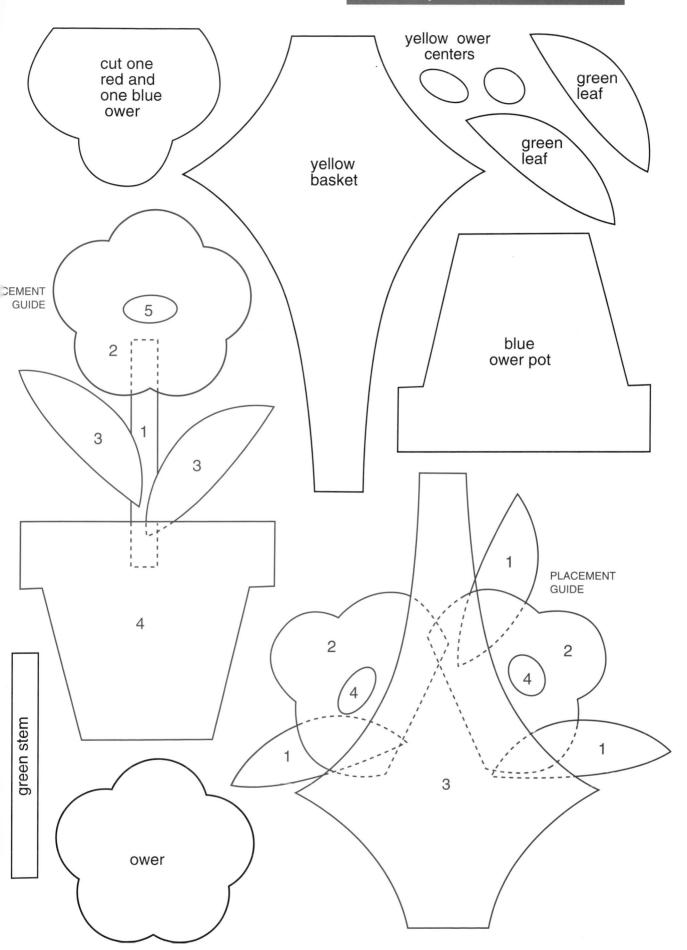

cut one
red and
one blue
ower

yellow ower
centers

green
leaf

yellow
basket

green
leaf

PLACEMENT
GUIDE

5

2

blue
ower pot

3

1

3

4

1

PLACEMENT
GUIDE

2

2

4

4

green stem

1

1

3

ower

made
by
Brenda
Henning

ABOUT PERKY POSIES

Brenda used various bright fabrics that have a lot of color and texture changes in them when designing this cheerful stained glass table runner. These fabrics add so much dimension to the flowers and leaves. She chose a high contrasting dark blue background to separate the red, pink, yellow, and orange border triangles. Bright fabrics will glow on a dark background. The rainbow of colors in the Quick Bias Tape is perfect for the stem.

PERKY POSIES YARDAGE
Finished Size 20" x 48"

Clover Quick Bias Tape
7 yds. Rainbow

Posy Fabric
3 1/2" x 7" yellow flower center
8" x 14" bright petals
8" x 14" leaves

Piecing Fabric
1 1/2 yd. background blue

Brightly Colored Fabric
1/3 yd. of a single fabric
or 12 fat quarters

Backing 22" x 50"

Batting 22" x 50"

BEGINNER B

SHOPPING LIST

SP1 Peaky & Spike template set (templates A, D and E)
Stiletto
Fusible tear-away stabilizer or freezer paper
Permanent (sharpie) marking pen
Chalk marking pencil
Roxanne's Glue-Baste-It
Sulky invisible thread
Sulky variegated metallic thread (142-7029)
Edge joining foot
Open toe foot
R quilting foot
Light box
Low-loft batting

CUTTING INSTRUCTIONS

Step 1. Two different units are needed for the table runner (corner units and side units). The difference is color placement and straight of grain. Read all cutting and sewing instructions before starting.

Step 2a. To straighten fabric see page 4. Cut two dark blue strips 2 7/8" wide (fabric matches center background). Place strips on top of each other. Make sure edges are in line. Place template D on top of strips as shown so bias is on longest edge. Cut 28 dark D triangles.

Cut two dark blue strips 4 7/8" wide. Place strips on top of each other. Flip flop template E cutting pieces as you go. Cut 24 dark E's

Cut one strip 2 7/8" wide from 12 different bright fabrics (fat quarters). If you use only one fabric, cut three strips from selvage to selvage. If you use 12 bright fabrics, cut 6 D's from each. Cut 4 more bright D's for corner units. Cut a total of 76 bright triangles

Step 2b. Cut one dark blue strip 2" wide. Place template D as shown on top of strip. Long edge of piece will be on straight of grain when cut. Keep these dark triangles separate from ones cut in step 2a. These pieces are only used for corner units. Cutting pieces this way puts straight of grain on outside edge of table runner and keeps corners from stretching out of shape. See diagrams in step 1.

Step 3. Cut two 4 1/2" squares using A template. Cut one dark rectangle 12 1/2" x 40 1/2".

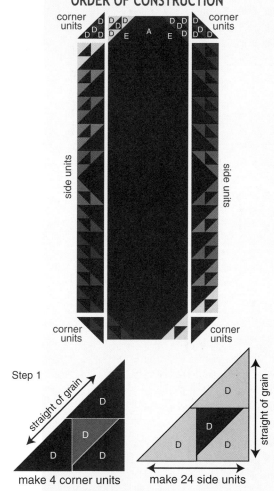

TABLE RUNNER
ORDER OF CONSTRUCTION

Step 1

make 4 corner units   make 24 side units

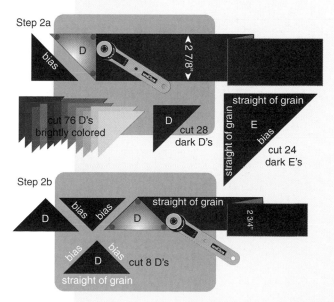

Step 2a

cut 76 D's brightly colored

cut 28 dark D's

cut 24 dark E's

Step 2b

cut 8 D's

Step 4.

anchor cloth

bias edges

D

D

do not backstitch

D

uneven seam allowance

anchor cloth

make 2 of each

Step 5

ears

90°

or

match corner of template to seam line

B

SEWING INSTRUCTIONS

Step 4. Take 2 D's from each bright fat quarter (24 total). Right sides together, join dark blue D triangles to bright D triangles. Identical shapes are easiest to sew together because there is no question about aligning them. Sew along bias edges. Do not back stitch at beginning or end of seam because it will be crossed over again. Guide pieces in front of presser foot with stiletto to prevent pieces from scooting to one side at end of seam.

Step 5. There are two ways to remove bulk in corners. With scissors, cut at 90° angle to outside edge of block before seams are pressed open.

With second method, finger press seam open. Place template on top of sewn unit and match corner of template to seam line. Remove excess with rotary cutter.

Two D's sewn together must equal the B square.

Step 6a

match corners

does not begin in crevice

D

b

D

D

D

1/4"

c

seam does end in crevice

D

D

match corners

bias

make 2 of each color for side units

straight of grain

make 4 corner units

Step 6a. Take one of the units made in step 4. Right sides together, place a matching bright D on top. Match corners indicated by arrow. This seam does not begin in the crevice. There will be a couple of stitches on the D. Do not back stitch at beginning or end of seam.

b. Finger press seam open. Intersection will be 1/4" from edge.

c. Right sides together, add another D. Match corners. This seam does end in crevice.

Make two of each color combination for sides.

Repeat step 6a - 6c and make four corner units using D triangles cut in step 2b. Straight of grain must be along outside edge to prevent corners from stretching out of shape. Set corner units aside until table runner is assembled.

Step 7

sew directly over intersection

1/4"

D

D

E

D

D

match corners

finger press seam open

4 1/2"

make 24 total

COMPLETING SIDE UNITS

Step 7. Trim off ears. Right sides together, add a dark E. Sew this seam with E on the bottom so intersection you want to sew over is visible.

Step 8

E

D

D

D

D

4 1/2"

4 1/2"

make 2 of each

Step 8. You get perfect points on right side if seam crosses directly over intersection. Each square should be a 4 1/2" square to match template A. Make two of each color combination for a total of 24 side units.

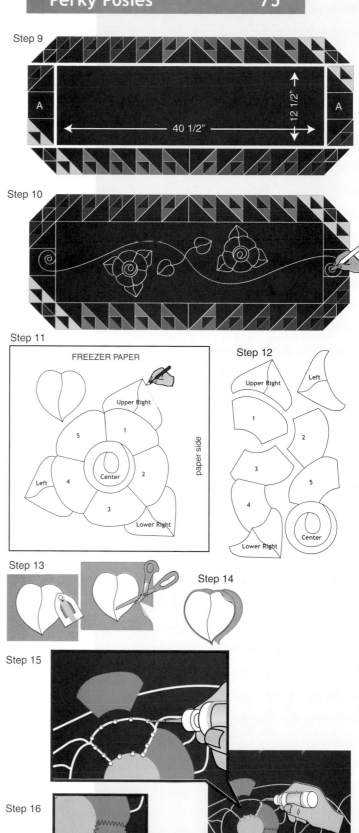

Step 9

Step 10

Step 11

FREEZER PAPER

Step 12

Upper Right

Left

5

1

Left

4

Center

2

3

Lower Right

paper side

Upper Right

1

2

3

5

4

Center

Lower Right

Step 13

Step 14

Step 15

Step 16

Step 9. Place an A square in center at each end. Turn side units as shown on each end before sewing together. Attach a corner unit to each end of side units. Press all seams open. Attach ends. Press seams open before adding sides. Press.

Step 10. If you have chosen to use a dark background fabric, like the model quilt on page 72, you may need to use a light box to transfer the design.

Center design under pieced table runner. Trace design onto right side of table runner using a white marking pencil. Do not transfer numbers from pattern onto table runner. Draw the stem by free hand after both flowers have been placed.

Step 11. Trace posy design onto paper side (not shiny side) of freezer paper. Label pieces by upper right or left and by number as indicated on pattern. These designations indicate placement of petals and leaves to simplify flower assembly.

Step 12. Cut freezer paper apart on drawn lines. These pieces will be your templates.

Step 13. Press shiny side of freezer paper to right side of selected flower fabrics using a warm iron. Cut fabric 1/16" larger than adhered freezer paper. You may layer fabric pieces right side up and cut multiple pieces at one time. Petals and leaves can be cut from two layers of fabric (both layers right side up) to avoid cutting each petal twice.

Step 14. Remove freezer paper from cut fabric pieces. The freezer paper templates may be saved and used again.

Step 15. Place dots of basting glue on pieced table runner along outline of piece to be positioned. Glue basting is shown using Roxanne's Glue-Baste-It! Carefully position fabric pieces on table runner. All dots of glue should be covered by applied fabric. Be sure that applique pieces are touching or overlapping slightly. Do not leave any gaps. Allow glue to dry.

Step 16. If this table runner is to be laundered, secure applique fabric edges with a zig zag stitch before applying the bias tape. This will prevent possibility of fabric edges escaping from bias tape and fraying. Brenda does not "wash" her stained glass quilts in a washing machine. It it needs to be cleaned, wash it in a sink or tub, treating it gently as you would a fine sweater. Blot to remove excess water and dry flat.

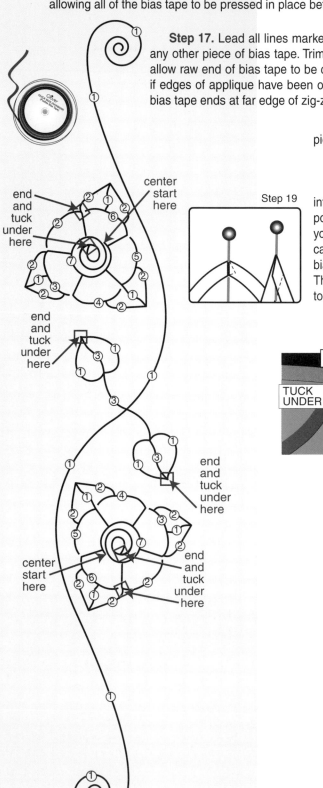

BIAS TAPE APPLICATION

The purpose of bias tape is to cover raw edges of all fabric pieces and to simulate stained glass leading. Bias tape is applied in a sequential order. The pattern has been numbered to make sequencing easier for you. Brenda uses Clover Quick Bias for all her stained glass quilts. Fusible web has been applied to wrong side of bias tape, allowing all of the bias tape to be pressed in place before stitching begins.

Step 17. Lead all lines marked #1 first. Bias tape lengths marked #1 do not cover raw end of any other piece of bias tape. Trim end of bias tape along leading line that is intersected. This will allow raw end of bias tape to be covered (overlapped 1/8") by next piece of bias tape. Notice that if edges of applique have been overcast with a zig zag stitch, bias tape covers all stitching! Trim bias tape ends at far edge of zig-zag stitches.

Step 18. After placing all pieces marked #1, place all #2 pieces, which will cover raw edges of #1 pieces, and so on.

Step 19. Miter bias tape at each point! Press fusible bias tape into place up to the point. Insert a pin into edge of bias tape where point of miter will be positioned. Pull bias tape against this pin as you fold under excess fabric, causing mitered angle to form. In case of a very sharp point, the fold may lay along outer edge of bias tape as shown at left. There must be no raw edges exposed. This cannot be emphasized enough. Brenda finds a stiletto useful to adjust the tape in front of the iron.

Step 19

Step 20. The pattern includes six bias tape intersections that are diagramed enclosed by a small box. This box indicates that the first piece of bias tape applied will need to be released from the design and another piece of bias tape inserted. Heat may be applied to bias tape to make it easier to lift.

Step 20

LIFT

TUCK UNDER

FINISHING TOUCHES

Step 21. Make a quilt sandwich by putting batting between backing and table runner. Thin cotton is preferred. Baste with safety pins and or basting spray.

Use Sulky invisible thread in top needle and in bobbin use thread to match quilt back. Stitch both sides of bias tape in place using a straight stitch along very edge of bias tape. Back stitch to secure thread ends. This quilts the table runner as the bias tape is sewn in place! Start stitching in center of table runner to prevent unsightly shifting of batting and backing. Brenda uses an open toe foot because this gives her an unobstructed view of the needle. If you have a Husqvarna Viking Quilt Designer, Designer II, or Designer I, use the needle stop down so the foot pops up making it easy for you to pivot on the curves and points.

See page 9 for instructions to bind the table runner.

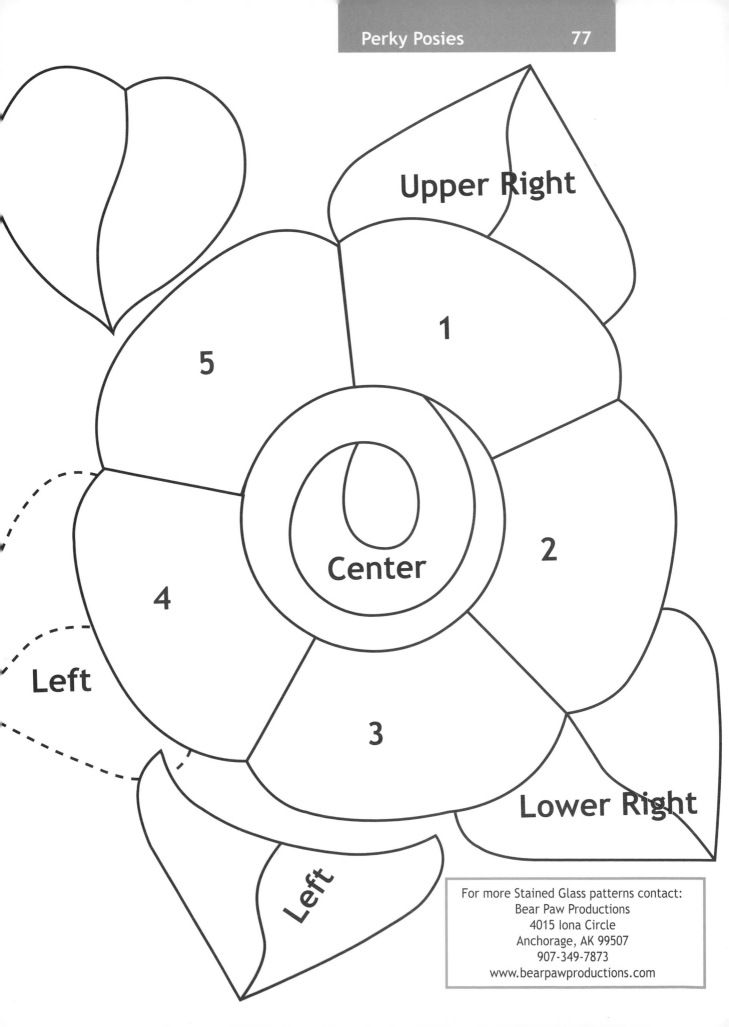

Upper Right

1

5

2

Center

4

Left

3

Lower Right

Left

For more Stained Glass patterns contact:
Bear Paw Productions
4015 Iona Circle
Anchorage, AK 99507
907-349-7873
www.bearpawproductions.com

Prairie Flower Yardage
finished size 51" x 51"

25 fat quarters for the main part of the quilt and wood pile border

1 1/4 yd. inside border, binding
1 1/2 yd. backing

designed & pieced by
Angela Scott

machine quilted by
Jean Johnson

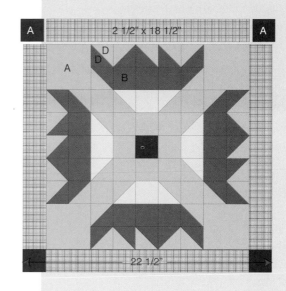

SHOPPING LIST

SP1 Peaky and Spike templates
QS 28 Log Cabin templates
Quick Grips
Small rotary cutter
Large and small mat board
Omnigrid® ruler 6" x 24"
Stiletto
Silk pins 0.50mm
Trans Web
Fasturn
Flannel Board

ABOUT THIS QUILT

This is Angie's version of a quilt pattern that four shops used for a shop hop. Each shop was given a black and white drawing and could use fabrics of their choice. Angie designed the quilt for *Quilting From The Heartland* with 25 fat quarters from one group of prints by Moda. Angie's palette includes 3 yellows, 4 purples, 5 greens, 2 reds, 5 creams and 6 tans.

The quilts weren't unveiled until the day of the shop hop. Four Cone flowers (one for each shop) form the focal point of the quilt. The wood pile border uses a variety of prints complementing the Cone flowers.

CUTTING INSTRUCTIONS

To Straighten fabric see page 4.

   Step 1. Peaky and Spike templates are used for cutting the Cone flowers in steps 1 and 2. Cut strips 2 7/8" wide for D's. Place template on top of strips as shown and cut number of pieces indicated in diagram. Bias is on longest edge of cut pieces.

   Step 2. Cut strips 2 1/2" wide for template B and 4 1/2" wide for template A. See diagram for number of pieces to cut of each fabric.

CUTTING WOOD PILE BORDER

   Step 3. Use Log Cabin templates for cutting the wood pile border. Layer 4-6 fat quarters on top of each other. Straighten and cut 1 3/4" strips. Because the wood pile border is scrappy and you need so few of each piece we cut only one set of pieces from each strip. The colors are evenly distributed in the border.

Step 1

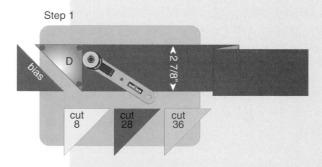

Step 2

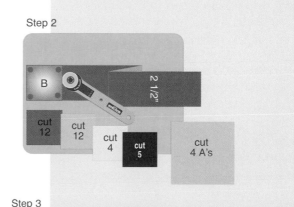

Step 3

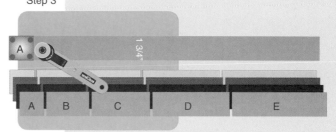

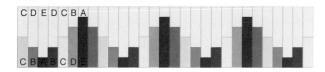

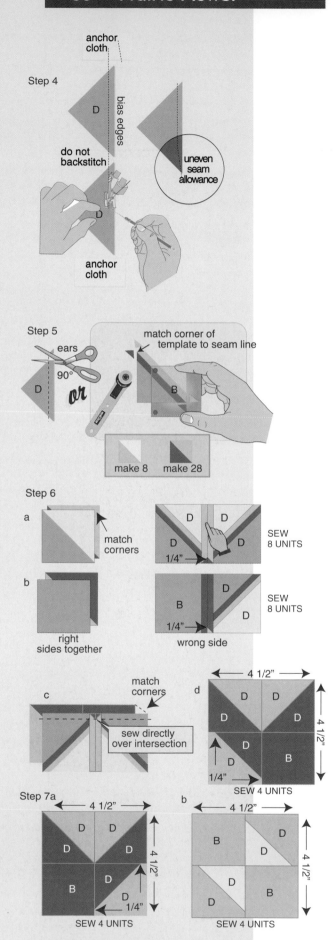

Step 4 — anchor cloth, bias edges, do not backstitch, D, D, uneven seam allowance, anchor cloth

Step 5 — ears, 90°, D, *or*, match corner of template to seam line, B, make 8, make 28

Step 6 — a, match corners, right sides together, D D D D 1/4", SEW 8 UNITS, b, B D D 1/4", wrong side, SEW 8 UNITS

c — match corners, sew directly over intersection

d — 4 1/2", D D D D B 1/4", 4 1/2", SEW 4 UNITS

Step 7a — 4 1/2", D D D D B D 1/4", 4 1/2", SEW 4 UNITS

b — 4 1/2", B D D D B, 4 1/2", SEW 4 UNITS

SEWING INSTRUCTION

Step 4. Arrange pieces on flannel board following diagram on page 79. First chain sew all half-square units. Place two D's right sides together. Identical shapes are easiest to sew together because there is no question about aligning them. Sew all seams with a scant 1/4" seam allowance (menu E-1 quilt stitch on Husqvarna Viking Designers). Sew along bias edges. Do not back stitch at beginning or end of seam because it will be crossed over again. If your machine eats fabric, start and finish on an anchor cloth. If you guide your piece in front of presser foot with a stiletto you don't have to worry about pieces scooting to one side at end of seam.

Step 5. There are two ways to remove bulk in corners. Cut at 90° angle to outside edge of block with a scissor or place a template on top of block after seams are pressed open and trim corners with a rotary cutter. If you are a beginner and your seam allowance is too scant, extra fabric can be removed with second method.

Step 6a. Put two units made in step 5 right sides together. Match corners and sew seam along light edge. Do not back stitch at beginning or end of seam. Finger press seam open. Press with iron. Intersection will be 1/4" from edge.
Make 8 of these units.

b. Right sides together, put a purple B on top of a D unit (purple and tan) made in step 5 (look at diagram for right placement). Sew along purple edge. Finger press seam open. Intersection will be 1/4" from edge (see arrow).
Make 8 of these units.

c. Place units made in Step 6a and 6b right sides together. See pinning techniques on page 6. Sew directly over intersection to get perfect point on right side. Finger press seam open. Press with an iron.

d. The block should be a 4 1/2" square. Check your block for accuracy by placing template A on top. Intersections should be 1/4" from edge.

Step 7a. Repeat and make 4 more units a mirror image of ones made in steps 6a-d. They should measure 4 1/2".

b. Make 4 units as shown using yellow and beige.

Step 8. On a flannel board, arrange units made in steps 6 and 7 on a flannel board as shown. Put an A in each corner. Make rest of units as shown to fill center of rows 1 and 5. Connect units to make third row as shown.

After all units are in place, continue connecting units into rows. Press all seams open before connecting the rows. Block should now be a 18 1/2" square.

Step 9. See diagram on page 79. Cut four strips 2 1/2" x 18 1/2" to frame center Cone Flower medallion block. Four red A's are used as corner stones.

Attach sides first. Sew these seams with strips on bottom so intersections you want to sew over are visible. Press seams open.

Attach an A to each end of top and bottom row. Add to top and bottom. Press seams open. The center medallion should now be a 22 1/2" square.

CUTTING CORNER TRIANGLES

Step 10. Cut two 16 1/2" squares. Cut them in half diagonally. Short sides are on straight of grain and long side is on bias.

If you want each corner fabric to be different, as shown in quilt on page 78, cut four 16 1/2" squares . Only half of each square will be used.

Step 11. Center bias edge of corner triangle on top of center medallion. There should be an ear at each end allowing for the 1/4" seam allowance. The seam begins and ends in the crevice. Press seam open. Continue attaching rest of corners.

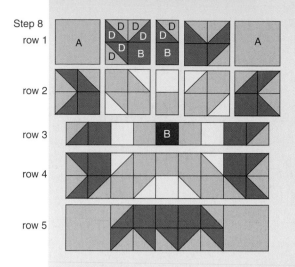

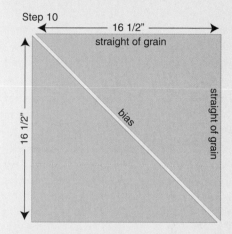

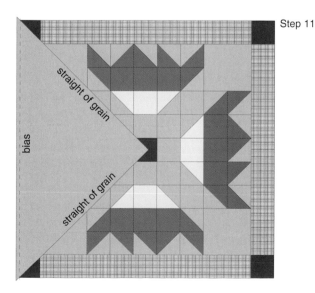

Step 12. The center square should now measure 31 5/8". Do not trim 1/4" seam allowance off outside edge after corner triangles have been added (see diagram); it is needed when adding outside border.

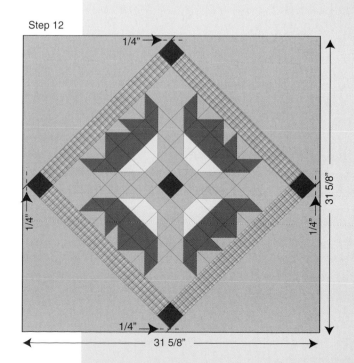

Step 13

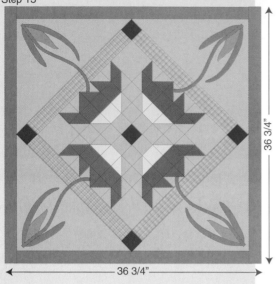

36 3/4"

36 3/4"

Step 13. Cut four 3 1/8" strips to frame the Cone Flower medallion. Attach frame to top and bottom first. Press seams open. Attach side borders. The Cone Flower block should now measure approximately 36 3/4".

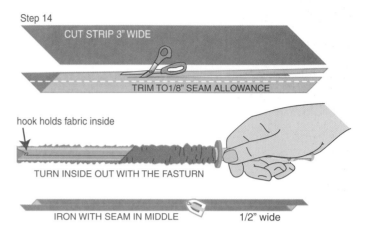

Step 14

CUT STRIP 3" WIDE

TRIM TO 1/8" SEAM ALLOWANCE

hook holds fabric inside

TURN INSIDE OUT WITH THE FASTURN

IRON WITH SEAM IN MIDDLE   1/2" wide

MAKING STEMS

Step 14. Cut strips for stems on the bias 1 1/2" wide. Fold fabric lengthwise right sides together. Sew 1/4" seam. Trim to 1/8" seam allowance.

To get smooth, flat seams, finger press seam open the first inch or two, as you start to turn the tube. The seam will stay open as you turn and it will be easier to press flat later.

Insert Fasturn tube. It is very important to fold 1/2" end of fabric over end of cylinder. Hold it tight, then insert wire hook in cylinder and pierce the fabric. More than 1/2" folded over may cause too much bunching inside cylinder as it is turned and may cause wire hook to tear out of the fabric. Pull bias tube back through tube. Press flat with iron.

APPLIQUÉ

Step 15a. Trace each leaf shape separately on smooth paper side of Trans Web or your favorite iron-on adhesive. Allow space between leaves.

b. Cut out each paper shape approximately 1/4" from drawing line. Press patterns onto back side of fabric.

c. Next cut out leaves following the drawing line on paper side of fusible web. Leaf applique drawings are in reverse of actual finished design.

Step 16. Peel off paper backing from applique leaves. Place cut applique pieces with fusible side down on background piece referring to quilt diagram in step 13. Remember to tuck any seam allowance behind shape on top of it. **Great tip!** Tap lightly with iron over applique. Hold up to see if you like placement. If you don't like the placement, you can lift the applique after it is cool if you haven't pressed too much. Fuse according to manufacture's directions.

Place a light weight, tear-away stabilizer under applique. Pin stem in place and attach with a small blanket stitch. Applique along edge of leaves with a small zig zag, satin stitch or blanket stitch.

Step 15

Trans Web or Iron-on adhesive

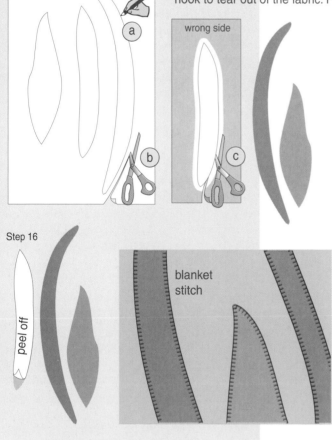

a

wrong side

b

c

Step 16

peel off

blanket stitch

WOODPILE BORDER

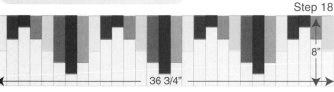

NUMBER OF UNITS TO SEW		
A	E	SEW 12
A	E	SEW 20
B	D	SEW 12
B	D	SEW 12
B	D	SEW 16
B	D	SEW 16
C	C	SEW 16
C	C	SEW 16

Step 17. If you make your border just like Angie did, follow this diagram for number of units to sew. Press seams open.

Step 18. Sew log units together as shown for woodpile border. Press seams open. Make four of these.

Step 18

8"

36 3/4"

Step 19. Follow order of construction to make corner units. Make four. Press seams open.

Add corner units to both ends of two woodpile borders. Next Attach woodpile border to two sides of quilt. Add top and bottom borders to finish the quilt top.

Step 19

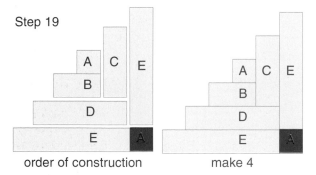

order of construction   make 4

Step 20. Place a ruler on top of the corners and trim with a rotary cutter.

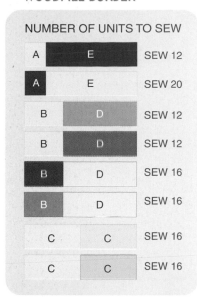

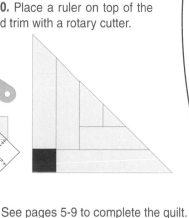

See pages 5-9 to complete the quilt.

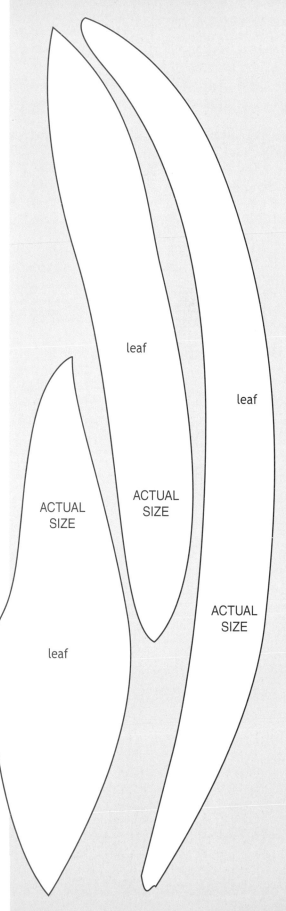

leaf

leaf

ACTUAL SIZE

ACTUAL SIZE

ACTUAL SIZE

leaf

leaf

DESIGNED AND
MADE BY

DEBBIE FIELD

FROM MY NECK OF THE WOODS YARDAGE
finished size 41" x 41"

3/4 yd. light

1 3/4 yd. dark
Outside border
and binding included

1/3 yd. Inside border

1 1/3 yd. Backing

APPLIQUÉ YARDAGE
1 fat quarter green for trees
1 fat quarter bear nose and moose horns
1 fat quarter moose head and bear body
1 fat quarter moose body

SHOPPING LIST
Peaky and Spike template set
Fabric Grips
Small Rotary Cutter
Large and small mat board
6" x 24" Omnigrid® ruler
Glass head silk pins 0.50
Stiletto
Open Toe Foot #412 27 70-45
Open Toe Stippling Foot #412 57 65-45
Heat n Bond or Trans Web
Light weight tear-away stabilizer
Low-loft batting

FROM MY NECK OF THE WOODS
Step 1. Debbie Field expressed her love of nature and the great outdoors in this wall quilt. Debbie chose fabrics with pine cones for the pieced blocks and outside border which were perfect for the theme of this quilt. She pulled the color for the inside border from the pine cones. Bear and moose appliques were combined with pieced blocks made with templates from Peaky and Spike. It is important to have a high contrast between the background and pieced work so the design doesn't get lost.

The pieced block measures 12 1/2" unfinished.

CUTTING INSTRUCTIONS
To straighten fabric see page 4.

Step 2. Cut 2 strips 2 7/8" wide of black print. Cut 2 strips 2 7/8" wide from white print. Place strips on top of each other making sure edges are in line. Bifold strips on a small mat board so it is easier to turn your work as you cut around the template. Flip-flop template cutting pieces as you go. The bias edge is always on the long edge of each piece and straight of grain is on both short edges. See diagram for number of pieces to cut.

Step 3. Cut a 4 1/2" strip from both the light and dark fabric. Place template A on top of strip and cut 8 light squares.

Cut 2 dark A's for center of blocks.

Step 1.

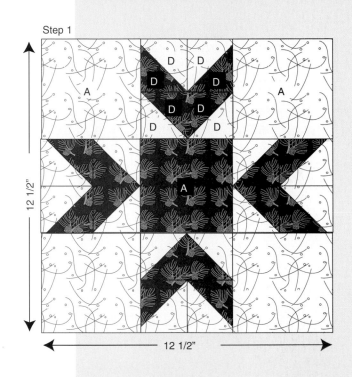

Step 2.

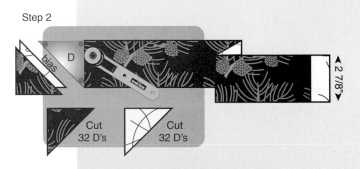

Cut 32 D's   Cut 32 D's

Step 3.

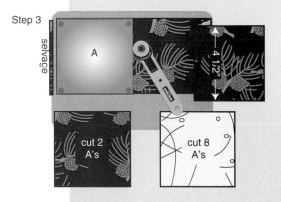

cut 2 A's   cut 8 A's

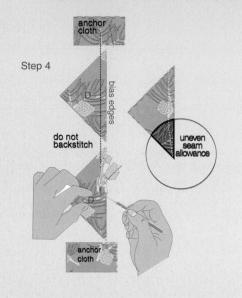

Step 4

anchor cloth

bias edges

do not backstitch

uneven seam allowance

D

D

anchor cloth

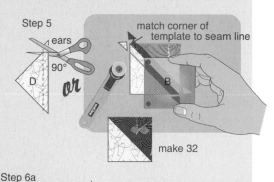

Step 5

ears

90°

D

or

match corner of template to seam line

B

make 32

SEWING INSTRUCTIONS

Step 4. Right sides together, join a light and dark D together. Identical shapes are easiest to sew together because there is no question about aligning them.

If your machine wants to eat fabric, start sewing on an anchor cloth; beginning stitches will be more secure and won't pull apart as easily as first stitches sewn.

To make up for fabric used in seam line, sew all seams with a scant 1/4" seam allowance (menu E-1 on Husqvarna Viking Designers). Sew along bias edge. Do not back stitch at beginning or end of seam because it will be crossed over again. Guide pieces in front of presser foot with stiletto to prevent pieces from scooting to one side at end of seam.

Step 5. There are two ways to remove bulk in corners. With scissors cut at 90° angle to outside edge of block before seams are pressed open.

With second method, finger press seam open. Place template B on top of sewn unit and match corner of template to seam line. Remove excess with rotary cutter.

Make 32 of these D units.

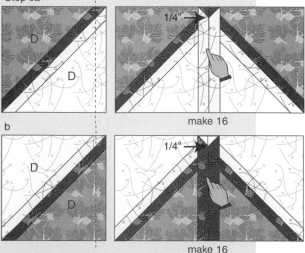

Step 6a

D

D

1/4"

make 16

b

D

D

1/4"

make 16

Step 7

1/4"

1/4"

Step 6a. Put two D units right sides together. Match corners. Sew along light edges. Do not back stitch at beginning or end of seam. Finger press seam open. Press with an iron. Intersection should be 1/4" from edge.
    Make 16 of these units.

b. Put two D units right sides together. Match corners. Sew along dark edges. Do not back stitch at beginning or end of seam. Finger press seam open before pressing with an iron. Intersection should be 1/4" from edge.
    Make 16 of these units.

Step 7. Put one of each unit made in steps 6a and 6b right sides together as shown in diagram. See pinning options on page 6. Sew directly over intersection to get perfect points.
    Make 8 of these units.

Step 8. Press seams open. Intersections should be 1/4" from edge. Each block should be a 4 1/2" square. Place template A on top of block to give yourself a sewing test.

Step 9. For rows 1 and 3, sew a 4 1/2" (A) square to each side of the unit finished in step 8. For center row, sew a dark 4 1/2" (A) square between two units as shown below. Press seams open.

Step 8

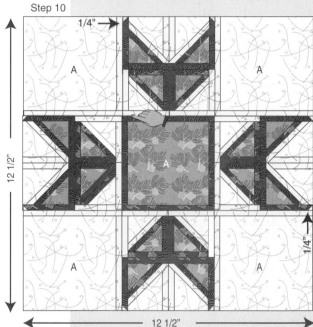

Step 9

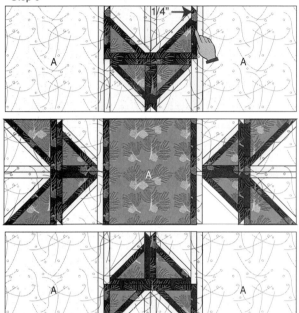

Step 10. Sew rows together to complete a block. Press seams open. The block should be a 12 1/2" square. Repeat to make 2 of these blocks.

Step 10

APPLIQUÉ

Step 11. Cut two 12 1/2" squares for background to applique designs. Trace applique shapes onto the paper side of Heat 'n bond or Trans Web.

Iron to wrong side of fabric.. Cut out shapes, peel paper off and position onto a 12 1/2" square. Buttonhole stitch or zigzag along edge of appliques.

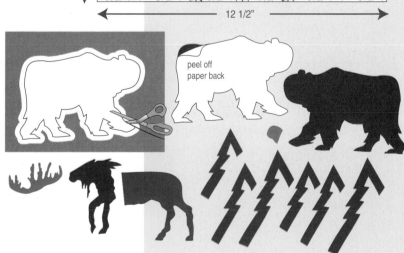

HEAT 'N BOND OR TRANS WEB

peel off paper back

Step 12

Step 12. Sew a 2 1/2" x 12 1/2" strip of sashing between pieced and applique blocks. Press seams open.

Sew a 2 1/2" x 26 1/2" strip of sashing between rows. press seams open.

Read pages 7-9 for border, quilting and binding tips.

Step 13. Cut four 2 1/2" strips from selvage to selvage for inside border. Attach to top and bottom. Press seams open. Repeat and attach borders to sides.

Step 14. Cut four 6" strips for outside border.

It is easy to adjust the size of this quilt. Just sew more blocks to make the wall quilt into a bed quilt.

FINISHING TOUCHES

To make the appliques and dark pieces stand out, Debbie meandered on all of the light background. She stitched around the appliques. The inside border has a continuous line loop pattern and the outside border was quilted with pine needles.

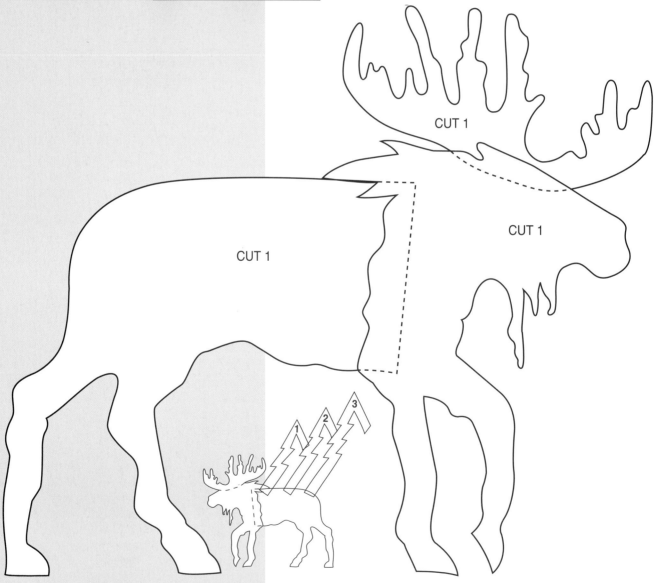

CUT 1

CUT 1

CUT 1

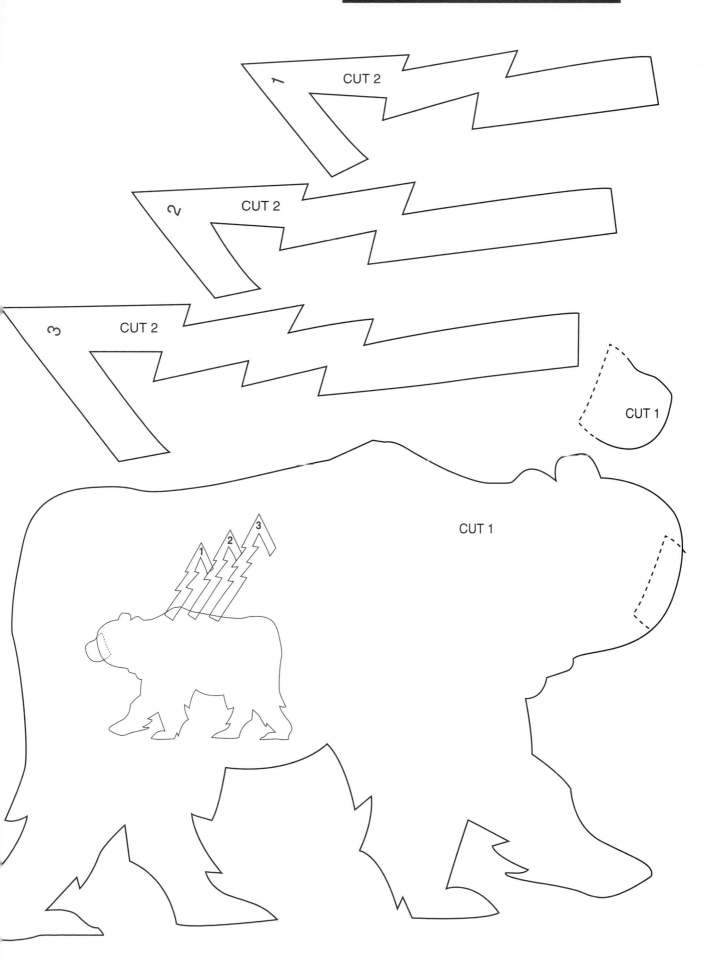

NORTHWOODS CATHEDRAL WINDOW *Finished size 30" 36"*

While not a true quilt, but a coverlet, the traditional Cathedral Window pattern was quite popular in the 1950s. Those unfamiliar with its construction are both intrigued and baffled by its complex appearance, however, once the technique is understood, endless, interesting variations are possible. Traditionally, muslin was used for the background blocks, but any good cotton will work. Heavier or thicker fabrics are poor choices due to the folding involved and the difficulty of achieving a sharp pointed corner. The windows are more versatile leaving fabric choices more open. Traditionally, the windows were filled with small squares of bright fabrics that resembled a stained glass window, hence the name Cathedral Window.

The Cathedral Window is based on a square unit and requires a minimum of two units to construct a window. Traditional Cathedral Windows used fairly small blocks and were worked entirely by hand. The small window area created by such small units does not allow enough space for most machine stitched embroidery designs. By using a 12 1/2" square of fabric, a window pane sporting a 2" embroidery design will not appear too crowded. The finished block will be half the size of the original block (after subtracting 1/2" for seam allowances) and the window pane area will be around half the finished block size. So a 12" block (after subtracting the 1/2") yields a 6" unit with a window area of approximately 3".

Cathedral window quilts are time intensive when constructed in the traditional method. However, the Northwoods quilt (shown above) can be constructed by machine and was completed in five days. What I like best about this quilt is that when the top is finished, the quilt is finished!

INTERMEDIATE

SHOPPING LIST

12 1/2" square ruler
Rotary cutter
Large and small mat board
40 weight Sulky® thread
Edge/joining foot
   (Husqvarna Viking 412 28 02-45)
Open toe foot
   (Husqvarna Viking 412 27 70-45)
Weblon stabilizer
Spray starch
Low-loft batting
Standard hoop 100x100 mm
   (Husqvarna Viking 412 44 70-01)
3" square from Quilter's Starter Kit

Cactus Punch Embroidery Design Collection
CC03 - Shar's Quilt
SIG05 - Holiday Trapunto
SIG23 - Snow Accessories
SIG 45 - Adventures with Fleece

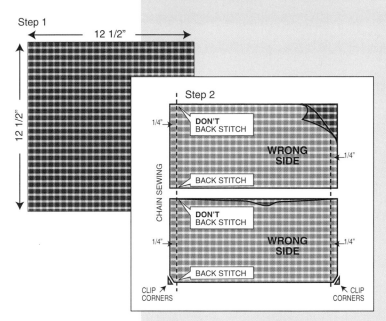

CONSTRUCTION

   Step 1. Using a 12 1/2" square ruler, cut as many squares as needed for your quilt. The quilt on page 90 uses 30 blocks arranged in a 5 x 6 grid.

   Step 2. Fold square in half, right sides together and sew each short end using a scant 1/4" seam with the open toe foot (menu E stitch1 on Husqvarna Viking Designer I, Designer II or Quilt Designer). Back stitch or tie off stitching at folded edge. The folded edge will become a corner point and will ravel out if not secured.

   Step 3. Finger press the seams open. It is easier to press this seam if the bottom part of the square hangs over edge of ironing board. Press only the seam (not the bias edges).

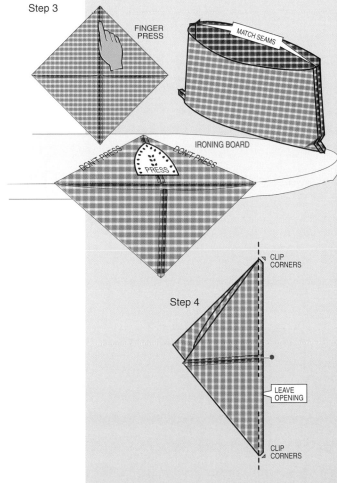

   Step 4. With right sides still together, match seams to each other and stitch across the top from one end and over seam about 2". Leave an opening gap of about 1.5" to turn and continue stitching to other end. Secure stitching at ends of stitching segments. Trim corners to reduce bulk.

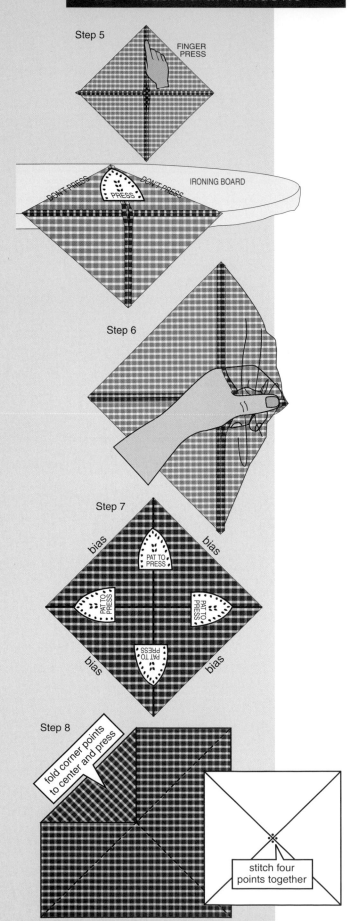

Step 5

FINGER PRESS

DON'T PRESS   DON'T PRESS   PRESS   IRONING BOARD

Step 6

Step 7

bias   bias   PAT TO PRESS   PAT TO PRESS   PAT TO PRESS   PAT TO PRESS   bias   bias

Step 8

fold corner points to center and press

stitch four points together

Step 5. Finger press seam open. Hang block over edge of ironing board and press seam open. Do not press bias edges. Rotate block and repeat pressing the opposite side.

TURNING THE BLOCK

Step 6. Insert your pointer finger into one of the points and put your thumb on the seam line as close as possible to the point. The thumb and pointer finger will be squeezed together. When turning block to right side, fabric will roll over tip of your pointer finger and your thumb nail will push the point out. Carefully encourage fabric to a sharper point with a pin before taking your thumb out. Repeat this step on all four corners.

You can also use a point turner to turn block.

Step 7. With seams up, press along seam line to corners to a sharp point. After pressing corners, press edges. The edges of the square are on the bias so press with care to avoid rolling or twisting. Whip stitch opening closed.

Step 8. With seam side still up, fold corner points to center and press in a crease. Make sure outer corners don't gap open.

There are two ways to complete the quilt so read rest of steps before continuing.

Whip stitch points together by hand or bar tack with sewing machine. Stitch points together. (A button attachment stitch works well. Menu B, stitch 16 on Husqvarna Viking Designer I, Designer II, or Quilt Designer). Adjust stitch width accordingly.

Step 9. Butt two squares together. Using an edge/joining foot, stitch blocks together using a lightning stitch (menu A, stitch 5 on a Husqvarna Viking Designer I, Designer II or Quilt Designer) or small zigzag stitch. Adjust stitch width to catch each block. Take care to match corners of blocks accurately. This stitching will be covered on front of quilt after window panes are inserted.

Step 9

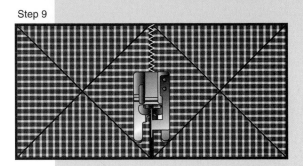

Step 10

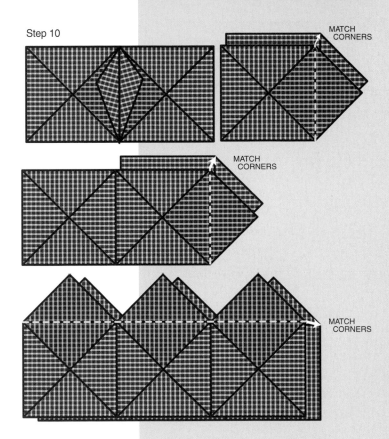

Step 10. With second method, **don't** connect center points (see step 8) before connecting blocks. Butt two squares up to each other. Lift a point from each square and match crease lines. Sew on crease to connect blocks. With this method you won't see zig zag stitch on bottom side. Continue connecting blocks into rows. Size of the quilt is determined by number of blocks in each row and number of rows you put together.

Next connect rows with same method.

Now go back to step 8 and whip stitch center points together or bar tack with sewing machine.

EMBROIDERY

The cathedral window quilt is a great way to showcase small embroidery designs. If you test sew designs on nice fabric, you may already have a ready stash of embroidered swatches that will work. Otherwise, you will need to select suitable designs and embroider on prepared fabric.

Designs on the Northwoods quilt required some editing and scaling to work at small size needed. Most animals were originally appliqués that were sewn with no appliqué fabrics inserted. Some designs, such as the upright grizzly bear were reduced in height from 7" to 2". Scaling this drastically, nearly always results in a disaster unless other changes are made as well. In this instance if you change the mouth to a running stitch and simply delete the claws (don't sew gray), you will be fine. As a rule, scaling designs up or down more than 20% will require some careful testing and results in a higher potential for poor results without editing.

Starch fabric before embroidering. Any tearaway backing used would likely show through any place it was not thoroughly picked away—a daunting task with all those tiny crevasses.

The Northwoods designs were embroidered on starched fabric squares that were hooped with a square of batting and a layer of "Soft N Sheer" for backing. This stabilizer is a very soft, lightweight cutaway that provides a smoother layer next to the machine and prevents possible snagging of the batting on the machine. Using this instead of tearaway saves production time since there is no need to remove the "Soft N Sheer".

See page 96 for complete details of where to find embroidery designs.

Designs used are relatively low stitch counts and use of few colors. The North Woods quilt uses a small color palette totaling eight different colors. To maximize your productivity, have a second hoop that you can be preparing while first hoop is in embroidery machine. Chances are you will need to cut your fabric much larger than your actual windows so that fabric can be properly hooped. The down side is that you can waste a lot of fabric but up side is that you don't have to be too particular about positioning your embroidery with fine accuracy. (See fabric-saving tip below.) You will use a template later to cut your window panes. If you have a round hoop, you may be able to cut smaller fabric squares for embroidery. When using a round hoop, I positioned my fabric on the bias (on point) in the hoop.

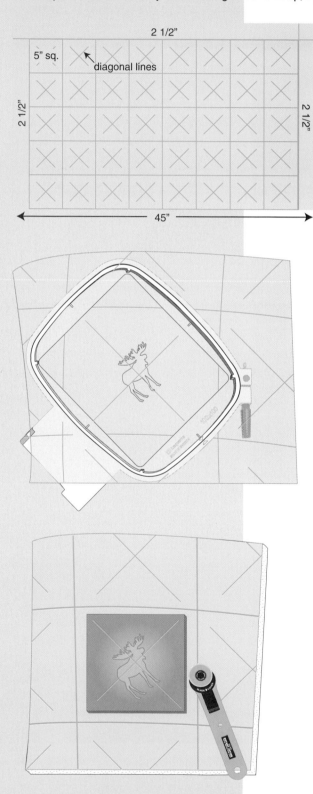

FABRIC SAVING TIP

If you want to save on fabric, make a chalk grid on fabric. Make a line 2 1/2" from the edge on three sides. Fill the center with 5" squares. Next, make two diagonal lines in the center of each square going from corner to corner. These lines are guides for positioning the hoop.

Make a quilt sandwich before hooping fabric. Put Weblon stabilizer on bottom, low loft batting in center, and gridded fabric on top, right side up. Cut a strip of stabilizer and batting 45" wide. Pin all three layers together.

Match diagonal lines on fabric to guides on hoop. Embroidered designs must sit on point to fit correctly in cathedral windows. While designs will be sewn on bias in hoop, squares will be cut on grain.

To cut panes to size, use 3 1/2" square from "Quilter's Starter Kit". If you don't have that template, make one from quilter's template plastic. Center template over your embroidered swatches and move it around until you are pleased with position. Most Northwoods designs had obvious horizontal and vertical directions. Fabric grain direction is not a big concern for this part. All squares for windows are cut so design is on point.

Step 11

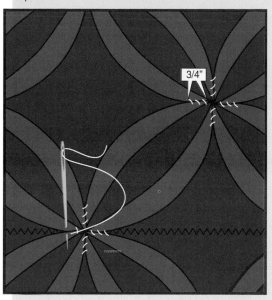

Step 11. To keep all points smooth and even, Lindee hand stitched corner points together down from each intersection 3/4" before inserting embroidered square. Use thread to match fabric.

Step 12. Pin a cut, embroidered window pane in space where two background blocks are butted up to each other. Fold edges of block over edge of window to form window frame; pin. These edges are on bias and fold over very nicely. Keep all edges even throughout your quilt. For example, maximum width on fold of window frame is about 1/2".

Step 13. Stitch around each window using stitch of your choice. Using open toe foot, Lindee chose a blanket stitch (menu F, stitch 11) with a stitch width of 1.0 mm. Don't forget to fold back and stitch frames along half squares around perimeter of quilt. Or, you may wish to stitch a bound border around outer edge. Lindee felt binding would detract from symmetry of the circular pattern created by folded window frames so she did not bind the quilt.

YARDAGE

Yardage seems like a lot but remember backing is also included. It took 3.5 yds. of background fabric for (30-blocks) Northwoods Animals quilt, which measures approximately 30" x 36".

If you want to make a larger quilt, add a 12 1/2" square for every 6" added.

If you are embroidering squares, base yardage calculations on block size needed for your embroidery hoop, not finished block size. You need 1 3/4 yd. for 49 embroidered designs. If you are cutting squares from a print you need only 3/4 yd. to fill windows.

Consider embroidering a label onto one of your background squares before stitching unit seams. Simply embroider in center of square and it will end up on back of block. Lindee likes to embroider her logo on her projects.

The layout below lists the source of the original designs used in this quilt. Since many designs were edited, Lindee has included the altered versions of designs from NAT01, NAT04, and CHO1 on CCO3.

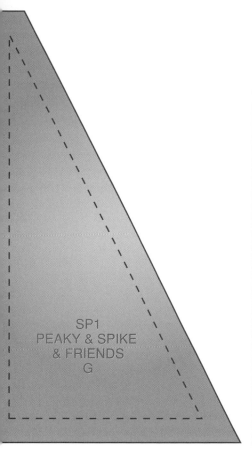

SP1
PEAKY & SPIKE
& FRIENDS
G

SP1
PEAKY & SPIKE
& FRIENDS
A

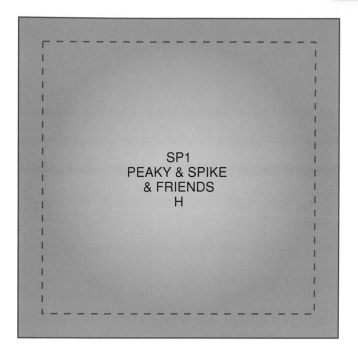

SP1
PEAKY & SPIKE
& FRIENDS
H

SP1
PEAKY & SPIKE
& FRIENDS
B

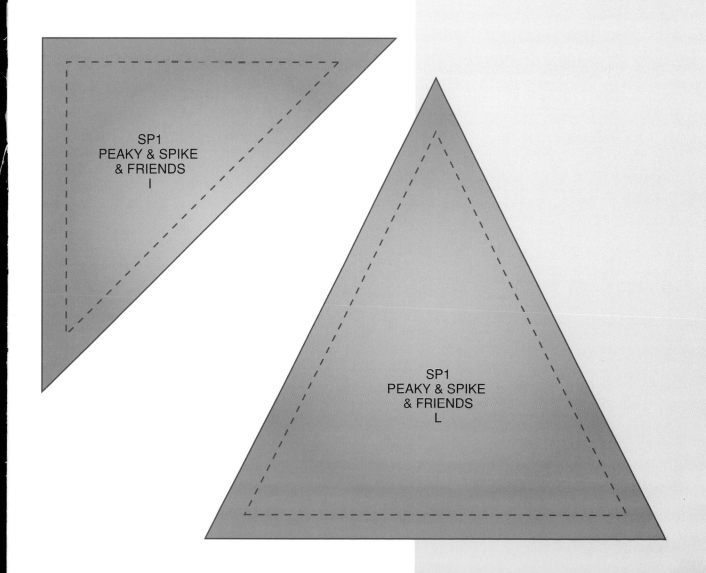

SP1
PEAKY & SPIKE
& FRIENDS
I

SP1
PEAKY & SPIKE
& FRIENDS
L

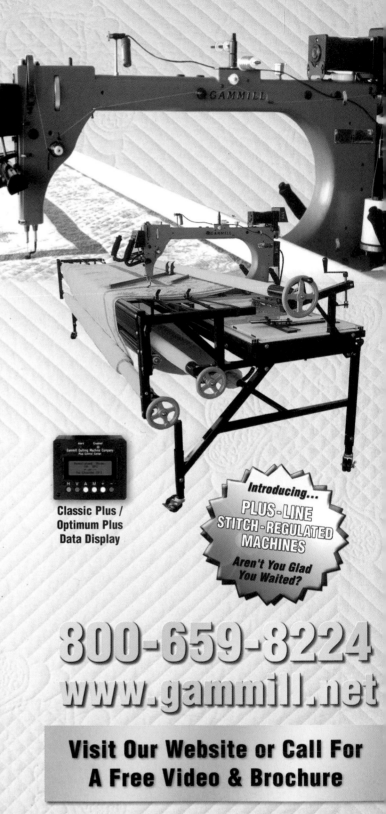

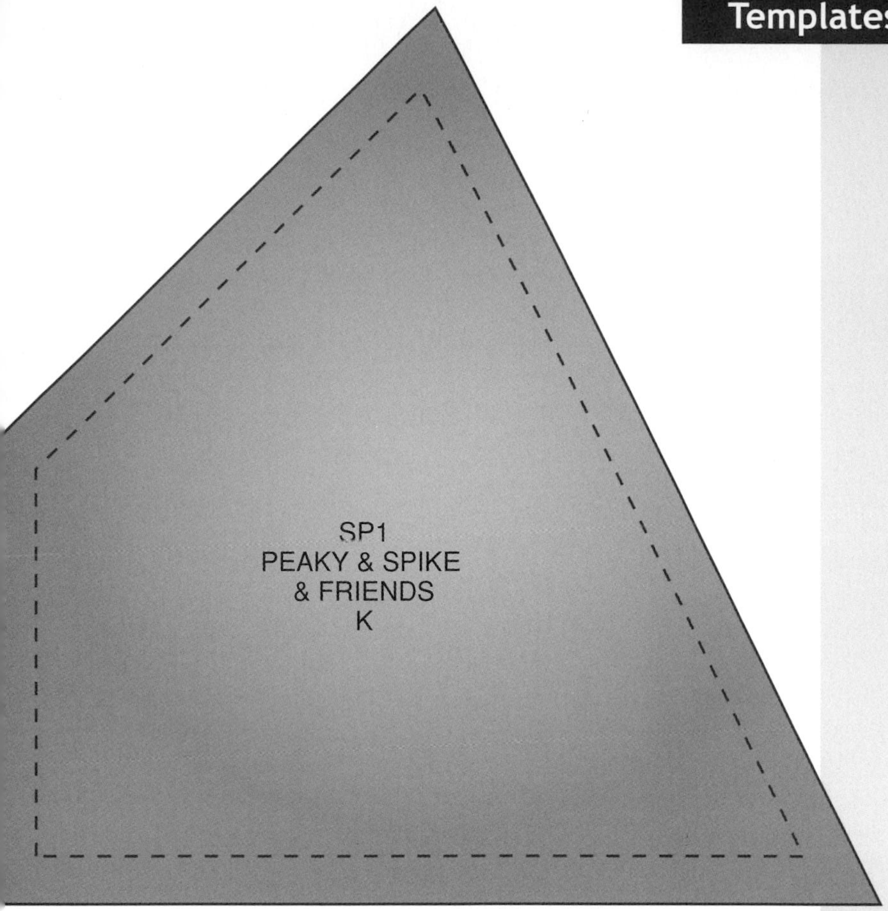

SP1
PEAKY & SPIKE
& FRIENDS
K

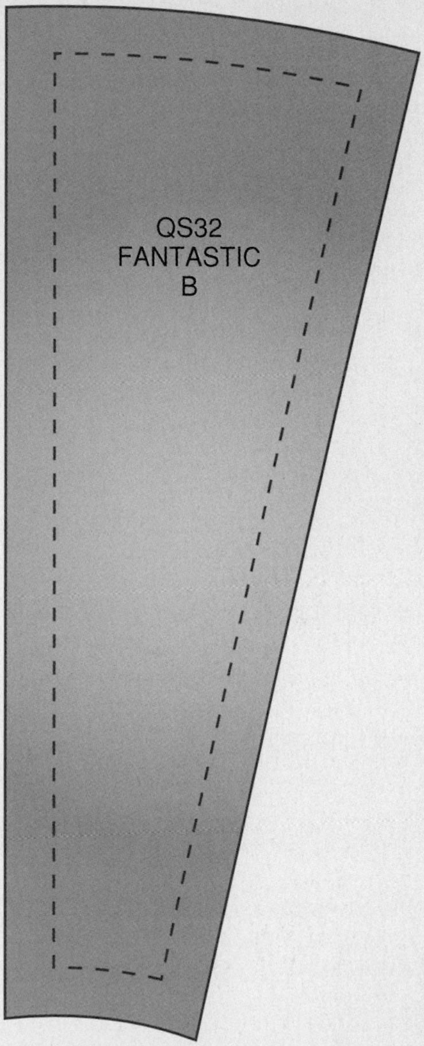

QS32
FANTASTIC
B

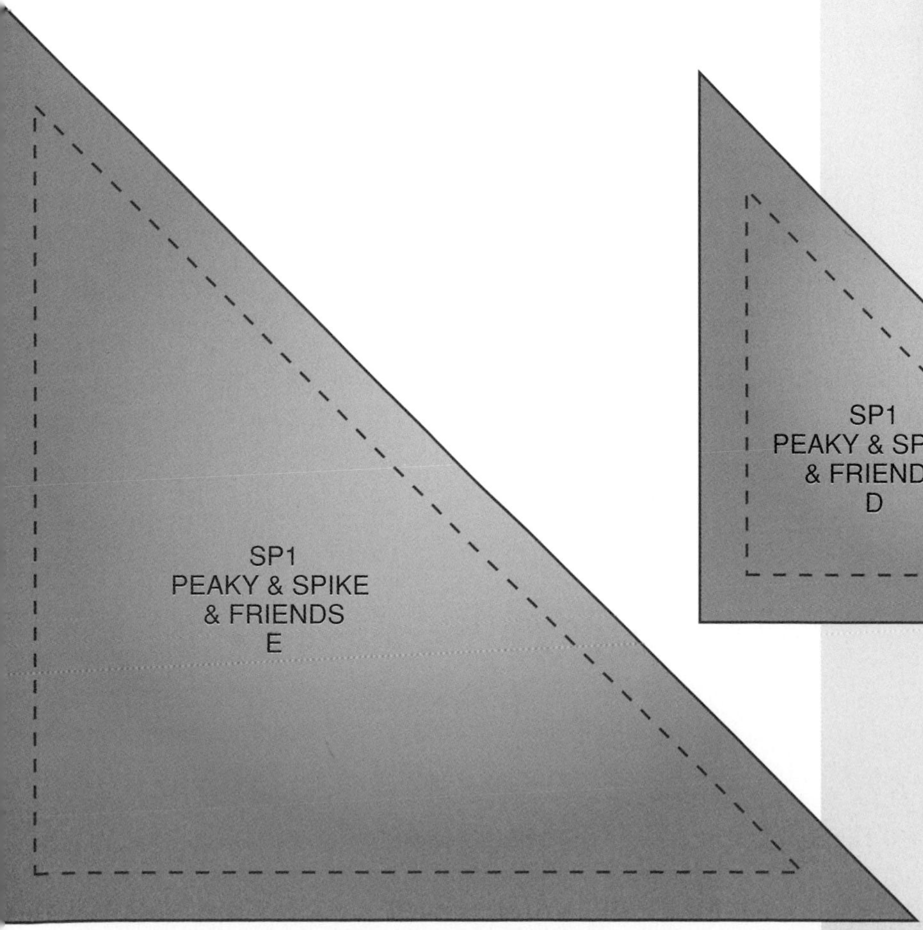

SP1
PEAKY & SPIKE
& FRIENDS
E

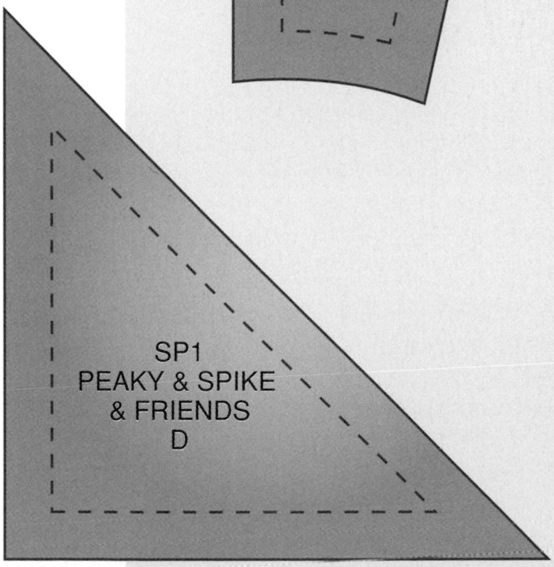

SP1
PEAKY & SPIKE
& FRIENDS
D

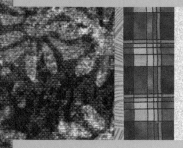